SARDINIA

DIVING GUIDE

WHITE STAR
PUBLISHERS

SARDINIA

Texts and photographs
Egidio Trainito

Illustrations and maps
Stefano Trainito

Editorial Coordination
Valeria Manferto De Fabianis

Graphic design
Patrizia Balocco Lovisetti
Clara Zanotti

Translation
Studio Traduzioni Vecchia

1 A carpet of jewel anemones (Corynactis viridis) covers the rock on the walls north of Secca di Su Puntillone . This is one of the most interesting natural sights in the waters of Sardinia.

2-3 Gorgonians, alcyonarians and golden zoanthids compete for space on the rocks of Secca del Papa.

4 top The camera flash reveals the bright colors of a red scorpionfish.

4 bottom Animals dominate in poorly illuminated areas: hundreds of organisms, sponges and gorgonians crowded on top of each other cover the wall at Secca Washington.

Contents

The author would like to thank:

Fulvio and Lodovica Poncini - Nautilus - Palau; Renato Romo and Giovanni Pinto - Centro Immersioni Figarolo - Golfo Aranci Cinzia, Roberta Calamita and Maurizio Uras - L'Argonauta - Cala Gonone; Marco Puggioni and Marco Foddis - Nautica Centro Sub S.Maria Navarrese; Vincenzo Sicbaldi - Airsub Service - Cagliari Andrea and Milena Vadilonga - Cagliari; Gianluigi Angius and Stefano Masala- Cagliari; Ornella Girosi and Gepi Caria Carloforte Tonnara and Isla Diving Center - Carloforte; Giuseppe and Mariangela Cappai + 1 - Malu Entu Diving - S'Archittu Vincenzo Piras - Bosa Diving Center ; Antonio Achilli and Alessandro Sirigu - Associazione Aquamarina Sassari Alessandro "Popi" Valoncini and Giovanni Messina- Diving Cente Costa Paradiso; Mario, Lalla, Pina, Monica, Claudio, Enrico Simona, Clara, Sara, Franca del Centro Sub Tavolara and al those who put up with me and supported me during this work.

STRAIT OF BONIFACIO

27

28

Maddalena island

26

CAPRERA ISLAND

PALAU

29

Mortorio island

Asinara island

25

30

GULF OF OLBIA

GULF OF ASINARA

2

Capo Figari

1

Capo Falcone

CASTELSARDO

4

Tavolara island

3

OLBIA

5

6

7

Molara island

SASSARI

MAR DI SARDEGNA

24

ALGHERO

Capo Caccia

Capo Comino

23

BOSA

OROSEI

8

22

CALA GONONE

9

GULF OF OROSEI

21

10

Capo Mannu

11

12

Capo di Mt. Santu

ORISTANO

13

ARBATAX

Capo Bellavista

GULF OF ORISTANO

Capo della Frasca

Capo Pecora

Capo Ferrato

GULF OF GONNESA

CAGLIARI

20

VILLASIMIUS

S. Pietro island

16

19

15

14

S.Antioco island

GULF OF CAGLIARI

TYRRHENIAN SEA

18

17

Capo Teulada

Capo Spartivento

INTRODUCTION

The fragrance of strawflowers, broom, rosemary and hundreds of other plants is the first thing you'll notice about the coast of Sardinia, even before your gaze wanders to the reefs and the long tongues of sand, and before your eyes are indelibly impressed with the dark blue to turquoise palette of colors that is the sea of Sardinia. It cannot be compared with any other tropical sea - there is something unique about it. Perhaps it is the transparent water, or perhaps the landscape in general. Another

water, on the limestone cliffs soaring 8 to 11 meters over the sea, the furrow carved by the waves 120,000 years ago is perfectly visible. And underwater, from quite shallow depths down to 60 meters deep, long ribbons of fossil beach are mute testimony to the slow rising of the sea level, which about 20,000 years ago was 120 meters below the current level. Geologists call them beach rocks, while Sardinians more colorfully and creatively refer to them as Roman roads, granites or brinks. Parallel to the present-day coastline are groups of conglomerate masses, a cracked and fissured mixture of sandstone and pebbles with generally only a few points resting

Sardinia
in the Mediterranean

Although the Mediterranean Sea is substantially homogenous from the biogeographical perspective, that is in the distribution of its forms of life, it is commonly divided into several distinct areas. To the west, the Alboran Sea, from the island of the same name located south of Spain, marks the boundary of and point of exchange with the Atlantic Ocean.
The western Mediterranean includes the central area from the Balearic Islands to Sicily. The Adriatic and the eastern Mediterranean are the other two areas that mark the northeastern portion and far eastern edge of the basin. Sardinia is right in the middle of the central Mediterranean, in a position which is universally considered conducive to creating a synthesis of the biological characteristics of the entire area. The origins of the species which now populate the Mediterranean can be traced back to the period in which all the continents on the Earth were part of a single enormous supercontinent called Pangea, into which flowed a deep gulf, the Tetide Sea. The Tetide Sea, located more or less where the Mediterranean is today, is considered the Mediterranean's area of origin.
It was a warm sea populated by large numbers of tropical species. Around that time, about 210 million years ago, the phenomenon of continental drift began: the great clumps of the earth's crust which are the present-day continents began to move, breaking the unity of Pangea and creating new seas. It required about two hundred million more years of continental drift to shape the Mediterranean into something akin to its present form. Around the end of this period, between 25 and 16 million years ago, the mass which now constitutes Sardinia and Corsica, almost a

A

B

sensation, not as immediate but just as strong, grows gradually as you sail along the coast of the island, and continues even when you dive underwater. It is the sign of passing time, of the enormous masses of water that have lapped, submerged and revealed the rocks and the sand that surround the island. It may seem a strange play on words, but the ancient name for Sardinia, Ichnusa, means "imprint," and the perimeter of the island does indeed show the indelible imprint of time. There are evident signs of the sea level pulsating against stable land where volcanic tumult ended far back in geological time. Thus, above

on the seabed, thus forming deep clefts. Like a dotted line that follows the entire perimeter of the island both above and below sea level, these signs of passing time seem proof that the boundary between land and sea is ephemeral, not only because it changes over time, but also and perhaps especially because underwater the landscape of the coast seems to continue unbroken.These underwater scenes, so impossible to capture by the limited technology of photography, remain indelibly imprinted in the memory of anyone who dives here, even more than the innumerable forms of life that cover them and swim around them.

C

D

microcontinent, broke off from the Pyrenean/Provençal area, forming the present-day Gulf of Leone, until it reached its current position. At the end of the Tertiary period, during the Pliocene between 10 and 17 million years ago, the Mediterranean was gradually closed off from the Indo-Pacific as the climate began to cool off. The first consequence of this process was the decrease in tropical species, and, with the increased isolation, the evolution of the remaining species to adapt to temperate waters.

At the same time, the drop in water temperature encouraged the arrival of numerous Atlantic species. During the Quaternary

These complex phenomena are the basis for present-day conditions, which make the Mediterranean a quite particular sea, where the only waters exchanged with the Atlantic are a superficial current flowing in and deep currents weakly flowing out. Compared with other areas of the Mediterranean, the sea that surrounds Sardinia is relatively stable, especially with respect to the waters of the open sea, which have a salinity level of 37-38%.

Even surface temperatures fluctuate consistently from 12 to 14 degrees Celsius in February and 23 to 25 degrees Celsius in August.

E

A - Wild rosemary in flower creates a delicate touch of color in the green scrub that covers the coast of the Gulf of Orosei.

B - In the spring, spurge flowers along the calcareous slopes of Tavolara.

C - Pancrazio illirico are wild lilies that flower among the rockslides and level areas. In the spring, the gullies leading to the sea along the eastern side of Tavolara become a garden of blossoming lilies.

D - The granite cliffs of the island of Mortorio, along the Gallura coast, include scrub areas swept by the mistral. The clear water makes it possible to see all the details of the sea floor.

E - A dune has been colonized by dense scrub on the island of Spargi in La Maddalena archipelago. Sand and rocks separate the green of the plants from the emerald green of the sea.

period, the Mediterranean, with Sardinia nearly in the center, had to a great extent assumed its present-day shape, and what most affected the evolution of the species in the basin was the progressive change in climate caused by alternating glacial and interglacial periods.

During cold periods in particular, the general system of currents changed, with surface waters flowing out of the Strait of Gibraltar and deep waters flowing in from the Atlantic.

This encouraged the arrival of so-called "cold fauna," or species of North Atlantic origin.

At present the sea around the island contains all groups of species typical of the entire Mediterranean.

Endemisms, which derive from Tetide Sea species, and Atlantic species, constitute the majority. Another important group is comprised of cosmopolitan species which are found in all seas on the planet.

Species with tropical affinities, which arrived during warm periods, are less numerous, and in the past hundred years, since the opening of the Suez Canal, some species from the Red Sea have also arrived.

Life in the sea

It is quite obvious that life in a marine environment develops differently from that on dry land. It is much less easy to understand the series of phenomena that causes this diversity, especially those which shape the distribution of organisms within the various environments. For example, the first problem we face underwater is how to determine what are plants and what are animals. How many times does someone say after a dive among gorgonians, "That was a amazing plant!" when in reality the plant component is absolutely secondary, as gorgonians, which appear to be

A

B

C

D

plants, are actually animals. We are accustomed to consider plants all those forms of life that are attached to the soil and have an arborescent form, while we expect animals to move, walk or crawl. The fact is that to obtain nourishment from the sea particular techniques are required which are closely bound to the medium in which the animals live. Indeed, even the most transparent water is full of living and dead organic matter that, carried by the waves, currents and tides, is continuously falling to the seabed. Thus, a great many animal organisms from various groups, even those quite distant from each other in evolutionary terms, have

developed specialized shapes and structures in order to capture this "manna from heaven." This explains why many marine animals are absolutely sedentary - because they have no need to go in search of food, just to catch it as it comes floating down.

It is clear, however, that for animals of this type, such as sponges, sea anemones, spirographs and ascidians, the presence of currents and more in general hydrodynamics, that is the overall movements of the sea, and the concentration of organic material present in an environment are all factors which affect their distribution.

Coming back to gorgonians, colonial animals consisting of a hard skeleton around which a connective tissue holds together hundreds of small polyps, in order to live and grow they need environments exposed to currents. Not only will we find them under these conditions, but the form and position of the colony will always be determined by the direction of the dominant current, to which they will always be positioned at a 90° angle in order to gather the greatest amount of food.

For plants, the primary conditioning factor is light. Indeed, plants do not eat other organisms, but grow by means of photosynthesis. They are thus capable of transforming simple inorganic substances (such as water and carbon dioxide) into complex organic substances (sugars), using light energy.

Thus the distribution of plants in marine environments is determined by the quantity and quality of light available. As sea water absorbs more light closer to the surface, especially the longer wavelengths, in the first few meters of water we will find primarily plants that utilize red wavelengths, while farther down there will be only those which photosynthesize with shorter green and blue wavelengths.

However, light is a factor that affects the distribution of animal organisms as well. In fact, many of them have nocturnal habits or are tied to zones with scarce illumination. In the dark zones, competition for space is also less fierce, because the plant component decreases drastically. A third element which also clearly affects the presence and quantity of marine organisms is the structure of the seabed. Using the various specialized structures they have at their disposition, both plants and sedentary animals find it possible to adhere to rocks and any hard substratum, and they both find it more difficult to adhere to sandy or muddy seabeds which continuously shift with the movements of the sea. Thus, these environments are colonized by specially adapted plants, such as marine phanerogams and oceanic Neptune grass in particular, while sedentary animals live for the most part dug in, with special adaptations which are interesting but much less visible and spectacular than those of animals that live in rocky areas.

A - Golden zoanthids and encrusting sponges cover the rocks. At first it is difficult to consider them animals, accustomed as we are to classifying anything that lives attached to the ground as plants.

B - A sea fan opens up from the rocks it has colonized. Don't be fooled by its plant-like form and the presence of flower-shaped polyps: sea fans are in fact colonial animals.

C - The sea fans grow on the shaded walls of Secca del Papa in numerous bi-color red and yellow colonies. This color variety is not common in the Mediterranean.

D - An alcyonarian extends its stubby branches from the rock at Capo Caccia. Unlike corals and gorgonians, the other animals of this group, alcyonarians do not have a rigid skeleton supporting the colony.

E - A group of rainbow wrasses surrounds a large white-tufted spirograph. This is an animal whose elegant appearance makes it hard to believe that it is in fact also a worm. The tuft is used for breathing and gathering food.

F - Coralligenous environments are complex areas where the animal component is predominant, including gorgonians, golden zoanthids and sponges.

G - The golden zoanthid is a cnidarian, an invertebrate with a simple structure. Its mouth is located in the center, and its tentacles with stinging cells at their tips are quite visible.

H - A moray peeps out of a hole in the rock, surrounded by golden zoanthids.

Underwater environments

One of the greatest attractions of the sea of Sardinia is its clear water. This is not just a question of appearance of what it looks like from the surface, or even of the colors under the rock walls or beyond the white beaches: indeed, at summer's end diving visibility in many areas can exceed 40 meters. But there are also less subjective elements that actually indicate the presence of clear water. One of these is the diffusion of broad, luxuriant meadows of Neptune grass growing all along the edges of the island, and which in less frequented areas are still almost completely intact. Neptune grass, which is a superior plant that, unlike algae, produces flowers and fruits and has roots and stems, colonizes detrital seabeds, and is usually not found at depths that exceed 40 meters. In many areas of the Sardinian coast, however, Neptune grass is found at considerably lower depths, for example in the Gulf of Orosei, where the exceptional transparency

B

C

B - In shadowy areas, red algae build projecting structures that change the form of the underlying rock and create an environment favorable for the growth of many other organisms. Neptune grass grows in the higher, more illuminated areas.

C - Some animals have exclusively nocturnal habits, like this beautiful berried anemone, Alicia mirabilis. Its long tentacles are completely retractable, and by day, when it is fully contracted, it becomes unrecognizable.

A

A - Neptune grass will colonize even rocky protrusions in illuminated areas. As the light decreases, the environment changes drastically, with explosions of color from red algae, sponges and other invertebrates.

of the water permits it to reach depths of over 45 meters.
It is generally agreed that the lower limit of Neptune grass meadows coincides with two other important limits. The first is the depth appropriate for recreational dives, which will also be used as a reference for the dives described in this guide. The second is the infralittoral band, which in the scheme used by marine environment experts runs from the average sea level to the edge of the circumlittoral band, which extends down to the edge of the continental plate, at a depth of about 200 meters. The division of the marine seabed into bands is useful in order to describe the distribution of the organisms that live in contact with the seabed, identifying zones in which ecological conditions are constant, separate from the bands above and below them, and in which biological associations change significantly. The dives described in this guide will all take place within the infralittoral band, where, in terms of quantity and diversity of species, the great majority of

marine organisms observable during dives are concentrated. The meadows of Neptune grass, one of the typical environments of the infralittoral area, are not popular with divers, but their apparent monotony actually hides an enormous quantity of life forms, so much so that that they are commonly compared with the Amazon forests. A dive on a meadow of this type certainly requires knowledge and a spirit of observation, but it should never be underestimated, especially when diving on mixed seabeds of rock and Neptune grass. Organisms from various groups hide at the base of the leaves. Many fish, including some quite large ones, also live right in the boundary areas between the rocky seabeds and the meadows. During nighttime dives you will clearly see how many forms of life emerge from the dense weave of Neptune grass leaves: sea urchins that migrate to higher levels, stupendous berried anemones, Alicia mirabilis, insignificant during the day, which distend in all their beauty, and fish and crustaceans

that appear unexpectedly.
The sandy or detrital seabeds are also given scant attention, although memorable encounters are also possible here, especially at night. It is quite a spectacle to observe a star-gazer which, almost completely buried in the sand, extends its tongue like a fishing line to capture small fish. But even by day, pearly razor fish, which dive headlong into the sand to hide, are alone worth a dive, as is the chance to observe the movements of the brightly-colored wrasses that perform their courting rituals on nests built in a field of caulerpa algae. The rocky seabeds are the classic site for dives both off the coast and in the open water, due to the variety of the seascape as well as the diversity of environments that can be experienced.
Photophilic algae, especially green and brown algae, which utilize longer wavelengths of light, are predominant on rocky summits and where direct light arrives. The reefs are covered by a soft layer of plants which varies in height and serves as pasture land for grazing species, especially sea urchins, which can graze down to the rock if there are no predators to stop them. Rough turbos, camouflaged by the layer of algae that covers even their shells, are also grazers. This is the reign of rainbow wrasses and green wrasses, but also of scorpionfish, predators with extraordinary mimetic abilities. In exposed areas slender colonies of hydrozoans undulate, and on them, drifting with the waves, are nudibranchs, predators specialized in the polyps of the host species. As you swim on the rocky seabed, you will immediately note how the composition of the organisms that covers the rocks changes with the varying quantity of available light. On the sides of the rocky masses facing north, on the steep walls, in the crevices and even in the smallest cracks in the rock, the pale colors of the algae shift suddenly to the red, orange and yellow of the sponges. The fans of the gorgonians stand out on the brick-colored red algae. The marc-colored sponges are speckled with the white and black of the nudibranchs. Carpets of golden zoanthids leave little room for red sea-squirts. The plant component

D

E

F

G

D - A small weever pokes just out of the detritus on the sea floor. Many predators live in sandy and detrital environments, hiding in the sediment as they wait to pounce upon their prey.

E - A small blenny searches for food among the algae that cover the rock. Blennies usually live hidden in cracks and holes. The tentacles on its head vary from species to species.

F - The cuttlefish is a cephalopod mollusk which is extremely common in coastal environments. It can change color quite rapidly to match the colors of the sea floor.

G - A small hermit crab (Dardanus arrosor) carries its shell on its back, covered with pink patches of encrusting red algae. The hermit crab uses its shell to protect its abdomen, which has no armor.

A - A small white grouper (Epinephelus aeneus) hides in a crevice among the rocks. It can easily be distinguished from the brown grouper due to its smaller size, lighter color and the light and dark stripes on its head.

B - A painted comber shows off its gaudy reproductive colors, which are brighter than normal, with the fine interweaving of red and blue lines on its head more evident, as is the blue spot on its stomach.

C - A triggerfish shows off its first dorsal fin as it swims. The fin can be retracted into a special compartment. The triggerfish is one of the most colorful fish of the Mediterranean, with complicated blue and turquoise patterns. Its colors change rapidly when the fish enters a new environment.

A

B

C

and annelids. The caves are a classic habitat for large and small crustaceans such as locust lobsters, spiny lobsters, common lobsters, porter crabs, banded shrimp, narval shrimp and *Herbstia condyliata* crabs. Brown meagres and groupers also live in the dark tunnels.

It may seem strange, but underwater in the Mediterranean the brightest colors are found where there is the least light, and this is also true of deep dives. In fact, there is an environment typical of the circumlittoral level, at depths of between 40 and 200 meters, where a flashlight may reveal groups of brightly colored algae and animals. This is the coralligenous area, characterized by concretions of calcareous red algae that build structures that change the form of the seabed or walls. Full of crevices, the coralligenous formations host a large number of animal organisms, many of which are brightly colored: the large red sea fans and the yellow branches of the sponges predominate. This is also where coral hunters seek out red coral, now at levels of over 100 meters deep, and where lobster fishing is concentrated. These are deep environments which divers may also encounter even at shallower depths, although they will be somewhat changed in composition. You may see coral formations, not as luxuriant as those in deeper waters, but still spectacular, even at shallow depths at the base of the cliffs and the cave entrances, on the reef walls exposed to the north in the open water and starting at a depth of about 30-35 meters in areas with less light. Often you will leave illuminated areas to enter coralligenous areas by passing through a transition zone where green algae such as sea cactus or sea fans predominate. The majority of the dives described in this guide are along routes that permit divers to visit the principal underwater environments and to clearly observe the transition areas between them. Here it will also be possible to observe characteristic plants and animals which in many cases are quite rare and which, along with the spectacular seascapes and the clear water, fully justify the fame of the sea of Sardinia.

decreases significantly in favor of animal species. Under the masses and in the cracks in the rock there is not only an explosion of color, but also of large fish, including groupers, brown meagres, seabreams and forkbeards, which also find shelter there. The dimly lit areas found among the rocks covered with photophilic algae are a sample of another typical environment, the caves. At cave entrances light decreases rapidly, and on the walls a succession of organisms can be seen, with the plant component progressively decreasing until it disappears altogether. The animals take the upper hand and completely

cover the rock, but even the animal presence decreases as you go deeper into the cave, until you reach the deepest crevices where the only light that ever arrives is your flashlight beam. Where there are no hydrodynamics, the rock is bare and you will only see animals capable of moving independently, primarily fish and crustaceans. Cave entrances are the preferred habitat for red coral, and along the northwest coast of Sardinia there are areas where this red gold covers vaults and walls only a few meters from the surface. Competing with red coral for space on the rock are stony corals, sponges, bryozoans

Going underwater

Of all the activities that involve close contact with nature, none is as enthralling as scuba diving, both because it takes place in an environment that can only be visited with the aid of special technologies and adaptations, and because the relationship with wild animals is so intimate that it cannot be compared with any other terrestrial environment - even in the Mediterranean. There is, however, a flip side to the coin, especially in areas where underwater tourism is increasing. Underwater environments are fragile, and often it takes only a moment to destroy an equilibrium constructed through years of slow growth. Here is an emblematic example: air, which for us is essential to life and which we carry underwater in our air tanks, is lethal to marine organisms. Simply by entering a cave or going under a vault, where the air we expel with each breath remains trapped, we can kill thousands and thousands of organisms that live clinging to the walls, in continuous competition among themselves for a place to live. Sometimes all it takes is a slap of your flippers or a hand carelessly placed to injure the community of organisms growing on a reef. Still, this is somewhat akin to the relatively slight damage that a run through a meadow may cause. But if a platoon of cavalry should ride through that meadow every day, it would soon become a bleak, dusty stretch of bare earth. This is the risk that the most beautiful and thus more popular diving areas face - that ill-considered visits will impoverish them. But precisely because of the physical conditions that distinguish them from land environments, marine environments themselves often offer a solution to the problem. Underwater it is possible to slip through the rocks and swim among schools of fish without making any physical contact, by simply imitating the fish and floating in the water. In fact, this very sensation of weightlessness, almost of abandon, is what some people most enjoy about diving. So what makes a diver a good diver is not physical strength, resistance or

the ability to go very deep. A good diver is aware of his or her own bulk, knows how to maintain a neutral position, and is capable of moving around properly in a marine environment, just as a good guest knows how to behave in someone else's house. Understanding and accepting the rhythms and balances of underwater environments are not just a way of keeping them intact, but are also the best way to enjoy their extraordinary beauty. One last comment: no one who goes for a walk in the woods fails to distinguish grass from trees, insects from berries or caterpillars from starlings. But how many people go scuba diving without knowing how to distinguish

a sponge from an algae or a worm from a mollusk? Too many. Yet knowledge is a fundamental prerequisite for preserving underwater habitats, and it is the best way to fully enjoy the complexity and diversity of the underwater environments of the Mediterranean and the sea that surrounds Sardinia. In addition to being a guide to the most beautiful locations on the Sardinian seabeds, this book should also be used as a tool for observing them from a different perspective, giving equal dignity to the majestic grouper and the tiny damselfish, to the famous lobsters and the microscopic nudibranchs, to the shining gorgonians and the disparaged Neptune grass.

D - Interesting environments can be found even at shallower depths. Here, just a few meters from the surface, the wall is covered with bright golden zoanthids.

E - By properly controlling position, divers can avoid touching the sea floor and at the same time reduce air consumption. The result is less impact on the marine environment and greater safety.

F - Underwater every crevice can hold a surprise. Familiarity with marine environments and the organisms that live there not only helps preserve them, but most importantly, improves the quality of every dive.

THE EASTERN COAST: FROM CAPO FIGARI TO THE GULF OF OROSEI

A long the eastern coast of Sardinia one element of the landscape acts as a common denominator: high walls of white limestone that terminate sheer to the sea. These are the remains of the great complex of sediments deposited during the Jurassic period and of which traces remain in some stretches of the interior as well. The calcareous coast has been greatly modified by the action of the surf, and many areas consists of active cliffs, where the action of the sea continues, in geologic time, of course, to weaken the rock at sea level, resulting in collapses and landslides that cause the shoreline to retreat inland.

In the more northern area, at Capo Figari and Tavolara, the limestone rests on the great granite foundation of Gallura, and the sheer walls are an exception in a landscape marked by the soft, smooth forms of granite. Descending south, the coast flattens and long tongues of sand alternate with rocky granite promontories. Basalt flows, the result of relatively recent volcanic eruptions, reach the sea near Orosei, and in the initial portion of the Gulf of Orosei they overlap onto sedimentary rock.

The coast of the Gulf of Orosei to Capo di Monte Santu is an enormous front of limestone with the mountains of Supramonte in the background. Here the beaches are small and set into vertical walls that delimit the ends of the *codule,* or dried-out riverbeds. The cliffs of the gulf are still active in only a few areas. Indeed, in many cases, just below the surface of the water at extremely shallow depths platforms of marine abrasion mitigate the violence of the waves and prevent the further retreat of the coast. Thus, while at Capo Figari and Tavolara the wall often descends more than 20 meters deep, along the coast of the Gulf of Orosei deep seabeds below the coast are found only in the southernmost portion. While these elements of geological homogeneity exist, in reality the landscape changes continuously on this stretch of the Sardinian coast, offering a wide variety of diving areas. Some of them have become classic Mediterranean dives.

Capo Figari offers dives on walls, rockslides and caves: every bit of the wall is good, and these are all environments with clear water where, in addition to the classic reef fauna, including the main attractions, groupers, brown meagres and lobsters, you may also see non-resident fish passing through.

There are numerous cavities, some of which are large and easy to explore, with the exit always in sight. The environment at Tavolara is similar, with a large number of diving areas which are primarily distinguished by the fact that within a depth of twenty meters you can find almost everything you ever wanted to see in a dive, except for coral. However, in this area the nearby islands of Molara and Molarotto, the other small islands, and the reefs and several shallows create a greater variety of underwater environments. Molara

and Molarotto are granite islands, and underwater the composition of the seabed is quite different from the limestone of Tavolara. Even the granite changes its appearance between the western side of Molara, with its rounded forms, and the eastern side and Molarotto, where the scenery becomes more dramatic, with spires and gullies. Descending southwards past Capo Coda Cavallo, the coast flattens, and underwater past the beaches, which become longer and more frequent, there are broad meadows of Neptune grass which gently drop toward greater depths. Across from Cinta Beach at S. Teodoro there is a vast complex of granite reefs; farther south, around the little

La città delle Nacchere

Il Mamuthone

Tedja Liscia

Secca del Papa

Secca di Punta Arresto

OLBIA

Secca to north-east of Molarotto

The Wreck of Molara

Secca di Osalla

The KT of Orosei

La Galleria

The Wreck of Cala Luna

island of Pedrami, there are other reefs. Shortly before reaching Capo Comino there is an entertaining and easy dive on the wreck of a Corsair, an American warplane, when the winter tides do not cover it with sand. Before turning to the Gulf of Orosei between Fuile Mare and Punta Nera, there is the secca di Punta Nera, formed by basalt flows that can even be seen on emerged land. There are more beaches at Marina di Orosei and Marina di Osala, then the coast suddenly rises, and from there until Capo di Monte Santu is dominated by limestone walls, with a myriad of enchanting cavities, caves and cracks riddling the mountain. Large karst phenomena have perforated the limestone, creating groups of enormous caves. The one that can be visited, the renowned Bue Marino cave, is only a taste of the intricate, amazingly long labyrinth of tunnels and grottos in this area, some of which open out above ground, and some underwater. This stretch of coast offers numerous good diving areas, many of which feature large, easily accessible caves at shallow depths. There is another common denominator for dives along this portion of eastern Sardinia - the presence of at least 12 modern wrecks, almost all of which are accessible to divers at depths no greater than 40 meters. Only the wreck of the *Klearcos*, which rests over 80 meters deep in the channel which separates Tavolara from Molara, is out of reach.

In 1979 the *Klearcos* was transporting a large variety of materials, including products containing arsenic, when a fire broke out on board. It soon burned out of control, and after several days of uncertainty and indecision on how to proceed, the ship sank between the two islands, taking its cargo with it.

In subsequent years some of the toxic materials were recovered. Nevertheless, divers who participated in the work do not tell tales of a polluted environment. On the contrary, it seems that the bridge of the ship has become a carpet of lobsters. A good sign!

C

D

E

F

A - The spire of Goloritzè in the Gulf of Orosei stands out on the small white beach against the emerald green sea. The cliffs of the gulf are interrupted only by the outlets of the codule, narrow, dried-out stream beds.

B - The arch of Goloritzè is one of the characteristic forms of the limestone on the eastern coast, where monk seals once lived. This legendary pinniped is now extinct in Sardinia due to ruthless hunting, destruction of its habitat and the invention of nylon nets.

C - The high limestone rock of Tavolara rises unexpectedly from sea at the end of the long beach of Spalmatore di Terra. Strawflowers are one of the principal pioneer plants that have colonized the coast

D - The bay of Capo Coda Cavallo seems to hold all the colors of the Sardinian coast. This photo shows an area which has been suggested for the establishment of the marine reserve of Tavolara

E - The Chrisso is one of many wrecks scattered along the east coast of Sardinia. It transported various goods and has been stranded on an emerging rock for about twenty years. Despite the shallow depth, this dive offers many interesting sights.

F - The wreck of the Corsair lies 6 meters deep on the white sand off Capo Comino. Often the tides cover it with sand, only to uncover it again later.

LA CITTÀ
DELLE NACCHERE

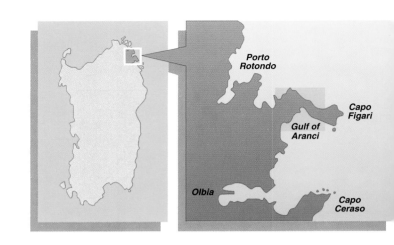

Porto
Rotondo

Capo
Figari

Gulf of
Aranci

Olbia

Capo
Ceraso

Gulf of Aranci

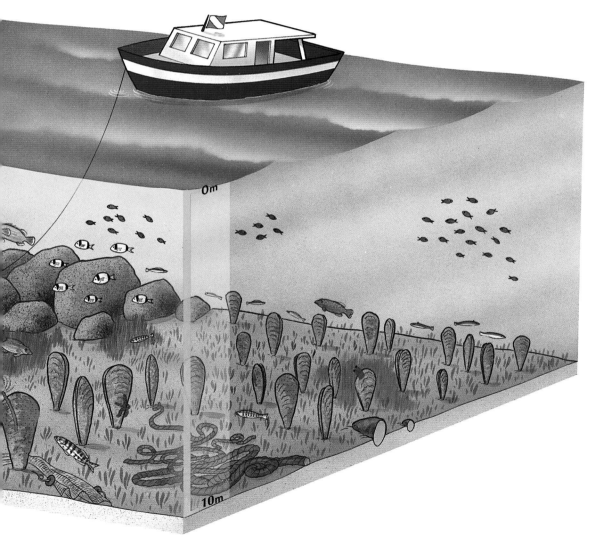

0m

10m

It is no coincidence that the first dive described in this guide falls outside the classic schemes. Indeed, it should be considered a declaration of intents, with the following fundamental values: naturalistic importance, the originality of the seascape and shallow depth.

Every summer, ferries run by the Italian State Railways and other navigation companies arrive at the Gulf of Aranci and unload thousands of vacationers, who in all probability have no idea that just a few dozen meters from where the ferry turns to pull up alongside the wharf, at a depth of only 10 meters, lies a rare bit of the history of the sea of Sardinia. Of course,

it's a rather special bit of history. An extraordinary population of *Pinna nobilis* is concentrated in just a few hundred square meters of space. Commonly called the fan mussel, this is the largest bivalve in the Mediterranean, and almost everywhere it is considered a species threatened with extinction. Illegal fishing practices, direct removal and environmental degradation have in fact enormously reduced its numbers. Yet at the Gulf of Aranci, hundreds of fan mussels stand out on a slightly muddy seabed colonized by green algae.

They are all quite old individuals, as testified by their length which, with great uniformity, is

C

A
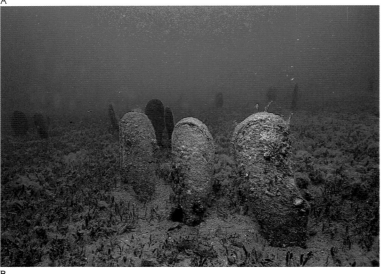

D

B

approximately 70 centimeters. They are all about twenty years old, and although many of them are dead although still standing, most are alive and well.

They are there almost as a testimony to the dramatic transformation of the seabed. And this is in fact what may explain their presence: in all probability the scattered spots of Neptune grass that can be seen among the fan mussels are the remains of a uniform meadow where, twenty or thirty years ago, the fan mussels began to grow. But while the bivalves grew the meadow retreated, as it has in many areas of Sardinia, due to the changes caused by increased human presence along the coast. And as often happens, the Neptune grass was replaced by caulerpa, a green algae typical of shallow, detrital seabeds. The most extraordinary thing is that this group of about one hundred fan mussels is still here, despite the fact that the bivalves continue to be fished everywhere and that signs of continuous human passage are evident. They have resisted nets, cables and anchors, and to see them still standing there seems almost an act of pride.

The dive is immediately surprising because the scenario is unusual: all those fan mussels on that flat seabed look something like the stones of an English cemetery. At first you wander at this depth, and it is natural to try to determine the extent of the area occupied by the bivalves. It is quite vast, and although it varies in concentration, the fan mussels are always quite dense. A few have been knocked over, and some on the ground are still alive. But there is another aspect of this dive: in this seemingly impoverished, almost bleak environment, each fan mussel acts as a condominium for thousands of other organisms from all animal groups.

Sponges, spirographs, ascidians and other mollusks live on their shells, seeking favorable spots. Even the dead fan mussels continue to function as receptacles: often wrasses make their nests in them, or scorpionfish hide in them, camouflaged and waiting for their prey to pass.

Sea perch and painted combers hide behind their shells in wait of prey. Octopuses try to make a hearty meal out of the fan mussels: by inserting a hard object between the valves, they can prevent them from closing and get inside them, where they can eat them in comfort. In a couple of areas there are accumulations of rocky masses where a large number of fish hide, even, quite unexpectedly, a lovely grouper. It may seem strange, but on that seabed just a few meters deep, one hour of diving slips by almost without notice.

E

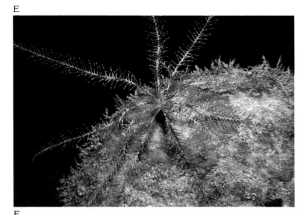

F

G

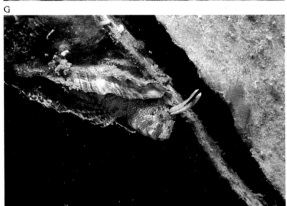

H

A - On the seabed, covered by a meadow of leafy caulerpa (Caulerpa prolifera), stand hundreds of fan mussels (Pinna nobilis). Similar sites can only be found in a few areas of Sardinia, as fan mussels are considered in danger of extinction.

B - Not all the fan mussels here are alive, but even those that have left only their shells host other forms of animal and plant life.

C - Sponges and spirographs have colonized the shell of a fan mussel. The movement of water created by the mollusk also brings food to its guests, thereby creating a favorable environment.

D - Algae (Acetabularia mediterranea) and oysters (Ostrea edulis) grow on living fan mussels. The elevated position offered by the shell permits the algae to receive more light and the oysters more food.

E - A crinoid (Antedon mediterranea) uses the position offered by a fan mussel to obtain food.

F - A blenny (Blennius tentacularis) uses the shell of a dead fan mussel as it awaits its prey.

G - A small blenny (Blennius tentacularis) lies in wait in an oyster attached to a fan mussel.

H - A small black scorpionfish (Scorpaena porcus) uses the shelter of the shell of a dead fan mussel to capture its prey.

IL MAMUTHONE

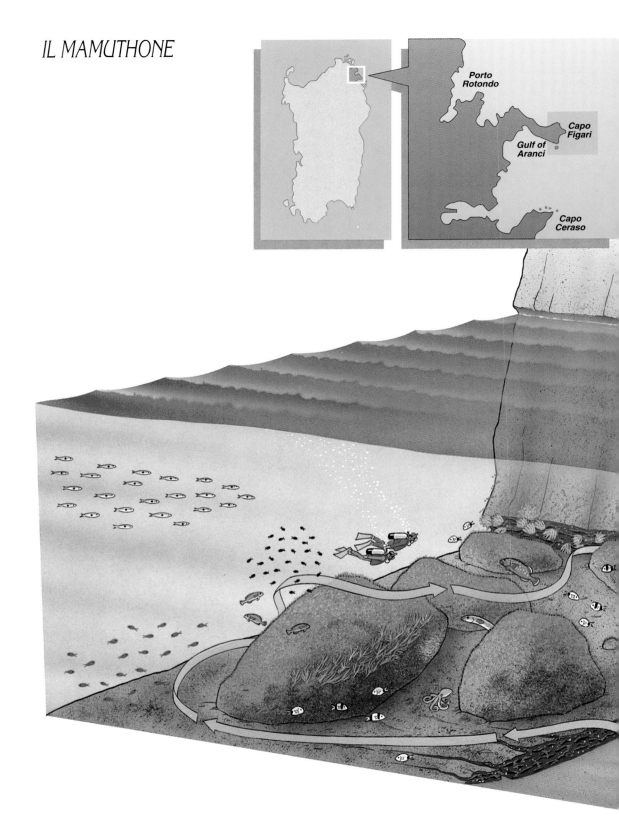

Porto Rotondo

Capo Figari

Gulf of Aranci

Capo Ceraso

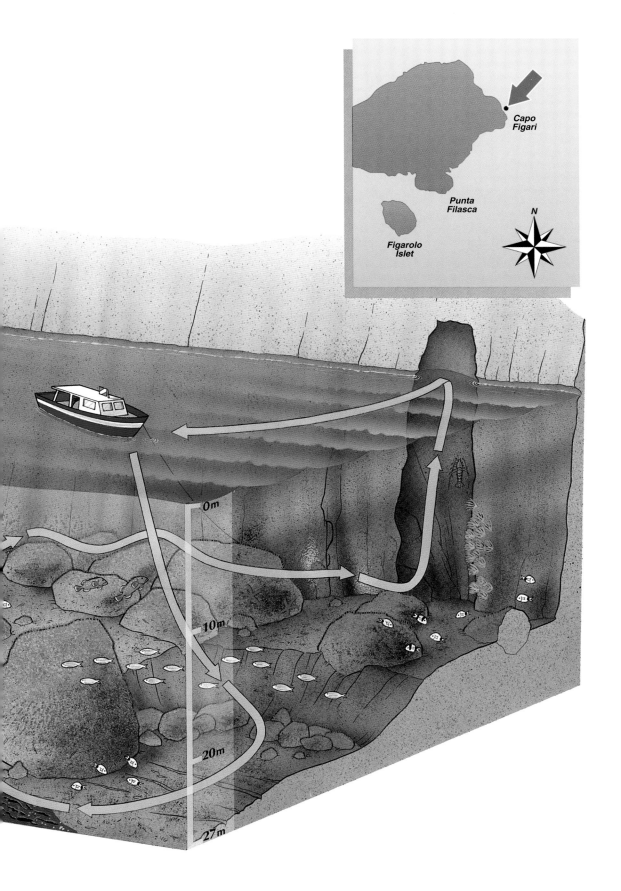

Capo
Figari

Punta
Filasca

Figarolo
Islet

N

0m

10m

20m

27m

A - The promontory of Capo Figari closes off the great Gulf of Olbia to the north. It is a piece of the limestone sheath that continues south from the island of Tavolara to the Gulf of Orosei. The cape slopes down toward the interior, while it juts out to sea with vertical walls.

Passing the tip of Capo Figari heading north, you come to a ledge in the wall facing the northeast. It is called Mamuthone due to the similarity of its profile with the Carnival mask of the same name from the city of Momoiada, in the Nuoro area. A little farther north the wall above the water has a large cavity called the Grotta Nera (Black Grotto). Anchor close to the wall over a mixed rock and detrital seabed about 24 meters deep. Descend along the mooring line and immediately head south.
The seabed slopes down gently to 27 meters deep, with coralligenous formations that cover low rocks. From here a slope of coral with

A

B

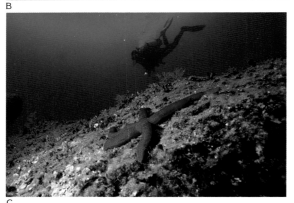

C

E

a jagged edge broken by fractures and gullies descends to a detrital seabed 35 meters deep. The more classic route continues among an accumulation of large rocky masses at 27 meters bathymetric line.
On the rocks there are bryozoans and small colonies of *Parerythopodium*. A large flat mass resting on the others forms a vault about 1 meter high, carpeted by stony corals (*Leptosammia pruvoti*). Several large brown meagres also swim in the dark: if you approach them carefully you will be able to observe them quite closely, keeping your flashlight off until the last minute. The meagres will retreat a bit as the light shines on them, but not enough to be out of sight.

B - Under the cliffs of the cape, the underwater environment shows the effects of reduced sunlight, and plants and animals typical of less illuminated areas predominate. A large red star (Ophidiaster ophidianus) with its gaudy purple color crawls through the algae.

C - Spiny lobsters, which are nocturnal creatures, live in the fissures between the rocks, even at shallow depths. They are generally small in size, as the larger ones now remain at great depths to avoid continuous fishing.

D - At the foot of the cliff, a projection forms crevices colonized by various organisms, especially animals. Sponges, cnidarians and bryozoans grow on a substratum of calcareous red algae. The low light creates habitats typical of deeper waters.

E - Yellow sea fans (Eunicella cavolinii) are typical of precoralligenous zones at the base of the cliffs of Capo Figari. The position of the fan indicates the presence of currents around the base of the wall.

F - Numerous cowries (Luria lurida) live in the dark caves and crevices. This mollusk covers its entire shell with its mantle, becoming quite mimetic. This cover is what makes its shell as bright as porcelain.

Around you, in the crevices and holes among the masses, numerous schools of anthias swim, each with its dominant male, larger and more colorful than the females.

Then ascend among the reefs where you can see a beautiful grouper, a conger eel, and swimming in the distant ocean depths, schools of seabreams and salemas. On the flat areas among the rocks you will see lairs of large octopuses, which are quite visible due to the accumulation of rocks and shells that marks the entries. Then ascend to the base of the rocky wall, where at about one meter from the seabed there is a horizontal ledge that follows the pattern of the cliffs. In the shadow of this canopy there is an environment typical of poorly illuminated areas, with golden zoanthids, bryozoans, annelids and sea fans that grow on a carpet of red algae. Follow the base of the wall and turn north to see another accumulation of masses where two beautiful groupers are hiding, not particularly intimidated by the approach of divers. Among the algae on the higher part of the masses a large red star (*Ophidiaster ophidianus*) is passing through, and all around swim lovely schools of salemas. Continue until you come to the masses located at the bottom of a wide crack 18 meters deep. This is an open cave that comes out of the water at a pronounced vertical angle and enters the wall in a V form. Right at the entry you can see a nice

I

J

G - Large red scorpionfish (Scorpaena scrofa) are common among the rocky masses on the seabed. Scorpionfish are predators that use mimicry and speed to capture their prey.

H - A conger eel (Conger conger) hides among the rocks, covered by large patches of encrusting sponges. The conger eel is a nocturnal predator with an elongated body. During the day it lives in lairs.

I - Brown meagres (Sciaena umbra) are quite common in the caves and crevices of Capo Figari. They often gather in dense schools at the entrances to their lairs, ready to retreat at the first sign of disturbance.

J - Octopuses, which may become quite large, are also quite common among the rockslides of the cape. Predators by night, by day octopuses tend to live in lairs, at the entrances to which they pile pebbles and shells which they use to block the entry.

F

G

H

group of brown meagres. Then enter the crack and go about 30 meters; the view toward the outside is quite lovely. Ascend up the walls of the cave with a first jump at 15 meters deep and a second at 3 meters. On the walls there is a classic succession of dark areas, where the golden zoanthids are gradually replaced by *Leptosammia cnidarians* until, in the more interior part, the presence of animals attached to the walls drops drastically. In the darker areas you can see cowries, lobsters and squills, while near the surface, where the hydrodynamics increase, the rock is covered with thick colonies of hydrozoans. After an entertaining safety stop which you can pass watching the small organisms that cover the rock, you'll surface over the deepest area of the crack, which exits on the outside and, after an initial portion with a low pyramid-shaped vault, turns into a broad opening where a rock arch separates the main entrance from a passage hole about 10 meters from the surface. The plays of light and shadow on the emerging rocks are quite beautiful, while the water is a deep turquoise blue. Come out of the cave and you'll be just a few meters from the boat moored right in front of you.

TEDJA LISCIA

Capo
Ceraso

Tavolara

Molarotto

Molara

Capo
Coda Cavallo

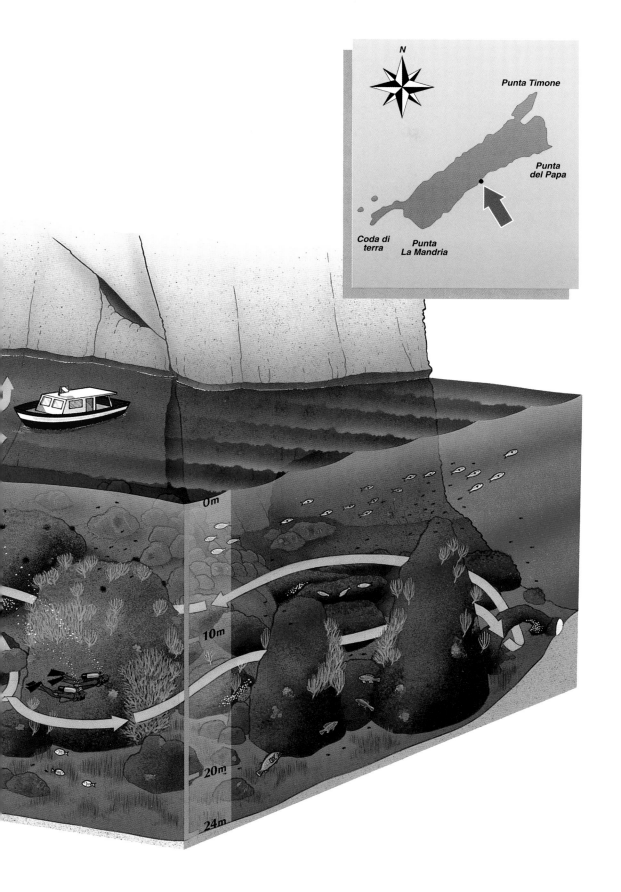

Punta Timone

Punta del Papa

Coda di terra

Punta La Mandria

N

0m

10m

20m

24m

A

B

C

D

The steep cliffs of Tavolara become less vertical for a short stretch along its central coast facing southeast, and right under an enormous mass that seems to be balanced on the wall is the island's most classic dive. Moor your boat off the coast on a wide plateau scattered with large rocks that rise from a seabed 10-12 meters deep to 5 meters below the surface. The dive can follow a number of routes. If you proceed perpendicular from the island towards the open sea, at 14 meters deep you will find the first pile of square rocks. The base of the rocks is at a depth of 22 meters. The seabed cover varies from thin, felt-like layers of photophilic algae to the typical

E

species of precoralligenous areas, where sea cactus (*Halimeda tuna*) and yellow sea fans (*Eunicella cavolinii*) predominate. The seabed slopes down gradually among scattered masses covered with sea fans on the outside portions, along with areas colonized by Neptune grass. At a depth of 27 meters you will find a vertical rock covered with Neptune grass. The depth increases to 36 meters, where the boundary with the deepest sandy channel is delimited by a series of large rocks that rise up to 3-4 meters from the surface. Here typical coralligenous formations begin, with a strong predominance of calcareous red algae. Along the route it is common to see large groups of white

A - Tavolara is a large block of limestone and dolomite located at the granite base of Gallura.
The southeast side, which offers the most interesting dives, is a long calcareous wall that drops vertically into the sea.

B - The rock on the almost vertical cliff forms a smooth surface, hence the name of the area (liscia means "smooth"). A view from above makes it possible to see the rockslides which characterize the seabed.

C - The large piles of rocky masses forms burrows, tunnels and crevices dominated by sciophilous organisms: a carpet of corals (Leptosammia pruvoti), sponges, annelids and bryozoans covers the vault of an easy passage.

D - At Tavolara there are signs of the karst phenomena which carved the rock when it was above water.
Often only brief stretches, such as this rock arch, remain of the ancient karst conduits on the seabed.

E - To the east is an area where the sheer wall blocks the light, resulting in rocks covered by organisms typical of precoralligenous areas: yellow gorgonians, red algae and sea cactuses.

F - Yellow sea fans are quite common at Tavolara even at shallow depths. They usually colonize passageways among the rocky masses where the conformation of the sea floor channels the currents, bringing food to these colonies of cnidarians.

seabreams, a few gilt-head breams and, when visibility is good, large dentex. At the base of the final rock masses are two large groupers: they remain stationary on the seabed or on smaller rocks, completely camouflaged. If you come too close they slowly but decisively head for their lair, but still leave you plenty of time to observe them. Your ascent to the surface takes place along a parallel route, and if you are wise enough to spend less time at greater depths, with the help of your computer, you should have plenty of time to visit the rockslides and crevices between the rocky masses on the shallower seabed around the anchor. Another shallower route parallels the coast at a depth of 20

G - In late spring, female locust lobsters (Scyllarides latus) deposit their eggs at Tavolara.

H - In early spring many large octopuses choose the rocks and crevices of Tedja Liscia for mating and depositing their eggs. During this vulnerable period their main defense is camouflage.

I - The summit of the masses is covered by a layer of green and brown algae. Salemas (Sarpa salpa) graze the algae in large schools. Often the group contains a number of "sentinels" who remain at the edge of the school without feeding, ready to give warning of any danger.

F

G

meters bathymetric line. At first you will pass the rocky masses of the first dive until you reach a passage between two large rocks. Here a vertical opening leads through a short tunnel among rocks and brightly colored coralligenous formations. You come out at a depth of 20 meters, where to your right an octopus makes its lair among the red algae almost every year. Continue, going around the largest mass, which outer side is covered with red algae, stony coral and gorgonians. At this point the seascape changes abruptly, as the overlooking wall becomes more vertical and reduces sunlight. The environment is of a precoralligenous nature, with a predominance of red and green algae typical of zones with less light. The calcareous red algae form mushroom-shaped structures full of crevices and arches, and under the light of your lamp everything appears brightly colored. On the dark red of the algae and the sponges the white and black colors of the nudibranchs (*Discodoris atromaculata*) stand out. A school of brown meagres moves slowly among the bases of the algae

formations and in the more open areas, while schools of salemas graze on the summits. In the center of this area there are two pyramid-shaped masses separated by a smaller rock. Below this is the den of a grouper, while on the shadowy walls it is not uncommon to see squills. Your return follows a shallower parallel route, skirting first the foot of the almost sheer cliffs which drop to 15 meters, and then passing a rockslide full of crevices where a small grouper often makes its den. You then reach the shallower water where the dive began, scattered with rocks where it is easy to spot octopuses, lobsters and, among the algae that cover the rock, camouflaged rough turbos covered with a coat of algae. Before ascending on the mooring line you'll have time to get a glimpse of the top of a rockslide that falls to a depth of 18 meters. Among the rocky masses on the seabed swim brown meagres and large, hard-to-spot groupers which are well camouflaged. As you ascend to the boat and during your safety stop, you'll have time to enjoy an overall view, in particular a large cloud of damselfish, always hovering above the highest rocks.

SECCA DEL PAPA

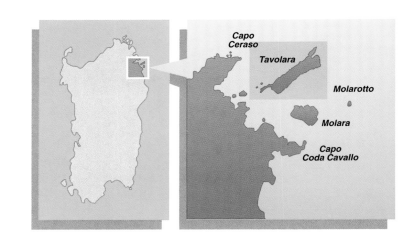

Capo Ceraso
Tavolara
Molarotto
Molara
Capo Coda Cavallo

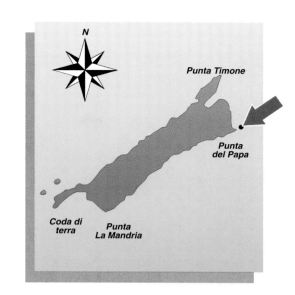

Punta Timone

Punta
del Papa

Coda di
terra

Punta
La Mandria

0m

10m

20m

30m

40m

R unning along the side of Tavolara that faces southeast, you will pass Punta del Papa, distinguished by a pinnacle that actually does look like a Pope wearing a papal tiara. Three hundred meters out to sea is Secca del Papa, a group of calcareous spires that continues the tip of the island underwater. The highest pinnacle comes to 15 meters from the surface, and you should anchor your boat here, on a little terrace about 3-4 square meters in size. The summit of the shallow is crowned by a cloud of damselfish, and often at the beginning of the slope you may see large amberjacks swimming. Follow the steep slope down to the west, heading toward a group of hills

A

do not make abrupt movements, you'll be able to get about 2-3 meters from them without causing them to retreat. Retrace your steps and pay attention to other details: a lovely school of white seabreams, a few morays, and many anthias. After you once again climb the main pinnacle, the second part of the dive unfolds on a route that offers a great deal to discover. Come to the northern wall of the shallow that descends vertically. Here, at a depth of 25 to 42 meters, there is a true forest of large sea fans: many are various shades of yellow, while others are red at the base and yellow at the tip. Often the branches of the gorgonians are colonized by an alcyonium, or leather coral, *Parerythopodium*

B

D

C

divided by deep troughs. You'll be swimming at a depth of about 28 to 30 meters, and you can see the large sea fans that cover the slope to the north of the masses. On the seabed at a depth of 38 meters there are large coralligenous formations that create tunnels and crevices. After passing the second spire, which is also covered with gorgonians, turn toward the third one. Even from about ten meters away, if you have a sharp eye you'll distinctly see the dark shapes of numerous groupers. You should go to the summit of the spire and wait. One after the other, 6 or 7 groupers will begin to approach suspiciously but curiously. Two of them are over 20 kg in size and are also less timid than the others. If you

A - Some of the sea fans (Paramuricea clavata) at Secca del Papa are more than one meter high.

B - At the extreme southeast tip of Tavolara is a limestone pinnacle that resembles a pope wearing a papal tiara; hence the name Punta del Papa. About 300 meters out to sea a group of underwater spires forms Secca del Papa.

C - Many areas of rock are covered by carpets of large golden zoanthids.

D - There are numerous gorgonians on the north walls of Secca del Papa.

E - A group of large groupers (Epinephelus marginatus) lives in the deeper area of Secca del Papa; they will often approach divers.

F - The yellow-red variety of sea fans is common only in a few areas of the Mediterranean; in Sardinia it can be seen at Secca del Papa.

G - Morays are common both in shallow waters and among the rocky masses on the sea floor.

H - Amberjacks (Seriola dumerilli) are pelagic fish which live in large schools, and the shallows out to sea are generally where they are most commonly observed. Groups of large amberjacks can be seen at Secca del Papa, especially at summer's end.

I - A nudibranch (Flabellina affinis), common on the Sardinian seabeds, deposits its eggs among the algae and hydrozoans of the top reef.

coralloides. Many other organisms live on the sea fans: bivalves (Pteria hirundo), annelids (Sabella spallazzani, Filograna implexa), and glass bell tunicates (Clavelina lepadiformis). Many areas of the wall are covered with carpets of large golden zoanthids. In the crevices swim groups of anthias. The dive continues with a spiraling ascent around the main pinnacle. At various depths there are little terraces: in the cracks live morays, conger eels and sometimes small groupers. Depending on the season, you may also see spinous spider crabs and porter crabs. On the summit sargassum grows, but is rarely able to attain any great height due to continuous grazing, especially by fish and sea urchins. The few specimens that manage to avoid the herbivores grow tall, supported by aerocysts, spherical bladders which act as a floating mechanism. Among the algae, hidden in the fissures of the rock during the day, there is always a long-spined urchin, a very elusive species difficult to spot. Due to its location in the open sea, Secca del Papa is one of the classic diving areas where one can expect to see large schools of pelagic fish. Large curious amberjacks, schools of big dentex and bonitos often choose the reef as a hunting ground, and if you are lucky enough to dive at the right time, you may be treated with unforgettable sights worthy of the best areas of the Mediterranean.

F

G

H

I

SECCA DI PUNTA ARRESTO

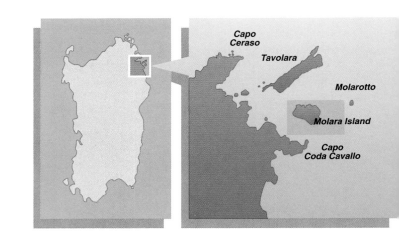

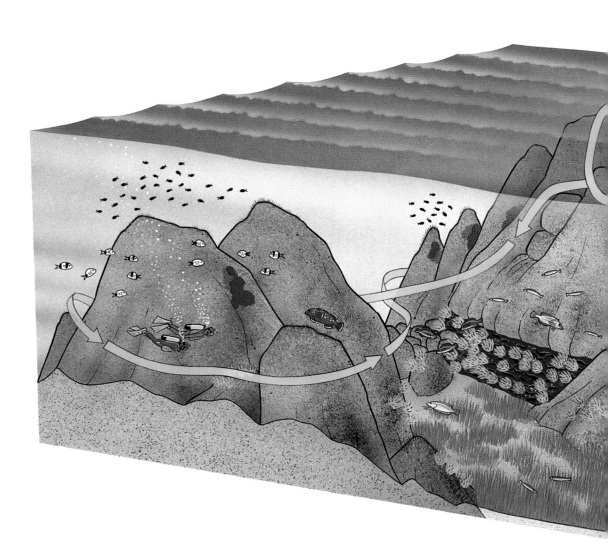

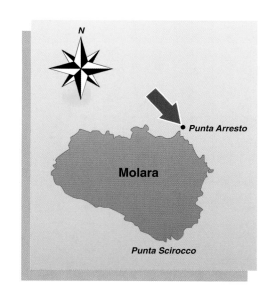

Punta Arresto

Molara

Punta Scirocco

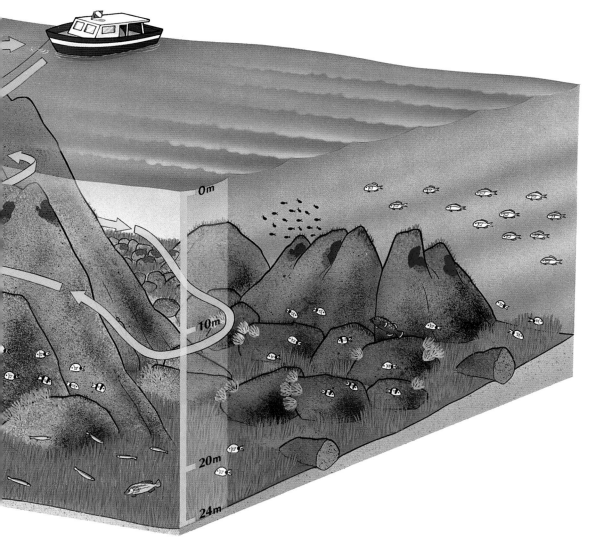

0m

10m

20m

24m

The northern side of Molara ends at Punta Arresto, a series of granite spurs that descend into the sea to the northeast. A few meters out from the point you can clearly see the glimmer of the shallow, which rises to 3 meters. It follows the form of the island, with its rocky ridges broken by deep troughs, as it continues below sea level, terminating at a depth of over 27 meters on a meadow of Neptune grass. Farther down, before the stretch of sand that covers the seabed at a depth of 36 meters, coralligenous concretions form a typical environment, with cracks, cavities and red algae formations. Head toward the open sea, entering the water along the first slope of the shallow. At a depth of about ten meters at the first pile of rocks, a grouper, little lobsters and a few squills may be in sight. At the end of the first jump, after passing a small rockslide right at the foot of the wall, you will cross a gully where rock masses are clustered, full of passages, *tafoni*, or cavities and passage holes. Here, beautiful brown meagres and a few forkbeards swim from one hole to the other.

Then head straight north in the direction of the gully at a depth of about 20 meters, until you reach the outer limit of the second bastion of rock. Following the rock to a depth of 27 meters, you will reach a trough with deep cracks, where brown meagres and often a pair of large

C

A

D

B

groupers swim. Ascend toward the summit of the rocks. Under the vaults and in the shadowy areas the purple red of the algae and the orange and azure blue of the sponges are spotted by yellow corals. You should always take a look around you, because anything may be swimming out in the blue depths. The only encounter with a dolphin I have ever been lucky to experience took place right here. In truth, the dolphin itself, a large adult bottle-nose curious about those strange, noisy creatures full of bubbles, was the one who came to inspect us. Materializing suddenly out of the blue depths, it came up to about two meters away from us, moving its head to get a better view.

It moved away a bit and then returned as if to take one last look, and then with a flip of its tail it was gone, vanished into the open sea. Although an encounter like this is a rarity, the same cannot be said for the lovely dentex and large seabreams. When you reach the summit, cross at the depth of the gully and move to the other side of the first group of rocks. Here there is a flat area covered by rock masses where you can see groupers and lobsters, and a stretch of smaller rocks almost entirely covered with algae from the genus *Codium* with a characteristic diffuse appearance. A grouper hides among the rocks and large wrasses swim about, and sometimes there may be some truly

large specimens of ballan wrasses. You then reach the ridge of the shallow and begin the ascent, following small gullies and spurs of rock where spirographs hover, until you come to the summit where the dive began. The safety stop is one of the most entertaining parts of the dive, and in fact you can wander among the rocks at a depth of 5 meters and discover a number of interesting things, including hermit crabs, nudibranchs and numerous spirographs. Swarms of rainbow wrasses and brightly colored ornate wrasses are always hunting on the rocks, and the final spectacle is the thick cloud of damselfish that covers the shallow and drifts rhythmically as the fish move in unison.

F

G

H

I

A - The island of Molara is formed of granitic rock. The surrounding seabeds are a combination of sandy areas, Neptune grass meadows and emerging rock.

B - The promontory of Punta Arresto juts out from the island to the northeast. The shallow is an underwater continuation of the rocks, characterized by square shapes.

C - The top of the shallow is a flat, tormented looking area, furrowed by channels and dotted with spires. A layer of photophilic algae grows on the rocks.

D - Numerous rocky spurs stretch out toward the open sea, separated by deep channels.

E - At the base of the rocks grow colonies of Eunicella singularis, which is easily distinguishable from other gorgonians by its greenish white color and its erect branches.

F - Often Neptune grass grows among the rocks, creating a habitat favorable for suspension feeders such as spirographs and sponges.

G - The painted comber is a predator that lives in constant contact with the sea floor. It is a common fish in this area, and its scientific name (Serranus scriba) comes from the interweaving of lines on its head, resembling ancient writing.

H - The black scorpionfish (Scorpaena porcus) is common in rocky areas of the shallow.

I - Salemas are quite common on the shallow: they patrol the rocks in large groups, grazing on the algae.

SECCA TO THE NORTH-EAST OF MOLAROTTO

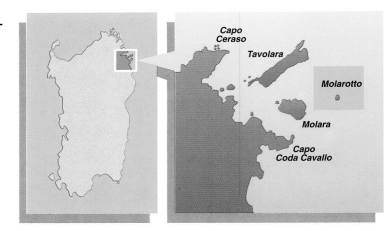

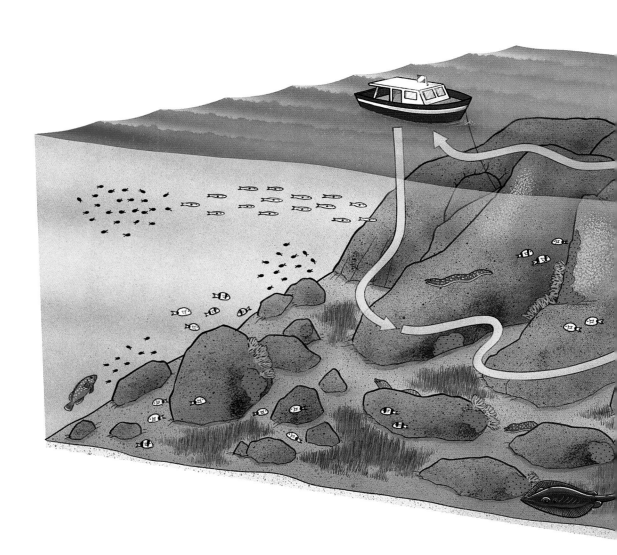

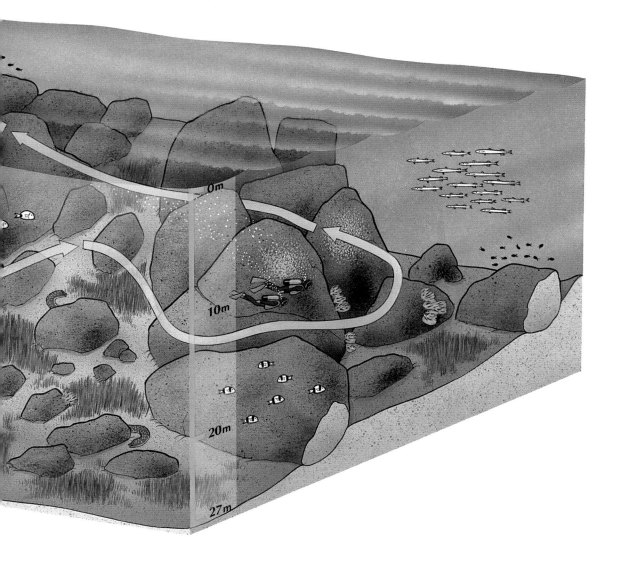

A

olarotto is a mass of
granite to the east of
Molara, around 8 miles from the
coast of Sardinia. It rises up to 51
meters above sea level and is
inhabited by a large colony of green
cormorants. During the mating
season, in winter and at the beginning
of spring, the cormorants occupy
every crevice among the rocks and
the sparse vegetation. Molarotto is
surrounded by a number of shallows,
rocky buttresses which run in various
directions to connect the emerging
rock with the seabed from which it
rises. The most classical dive is on
the northeast shallow. Moor the boat
over a bastion of rock that rises 9
meters from the surface. The dive
proceeds north, first skirting the base

B

D

C

of the four rocky ridges and then
returning along the higher portions
of the rocks. The ridges are
positioned in a northeast direction
and are separated by deep troughs
covered with rockslide masses and
patches of detritus. In the troughs
the seabed descends out to the open
sea from 18 to 24 meters deep at
the base of the rocks, then reaches
a depth of 27 meters, somewhat
towards the open sea. The rocky
bastions are covered with a felt-like
layer of photophilic algae, always
kept trimmed by grazing species
and by the strong hydrodynamics,
as the reef is practically in the open
sea. Indeed, currents are quite
common and must be taken into
consideration when planning the

A - Molarotto is a rock surrounded by numerous shallows that continue the forms of the emerged rocks underwater, with rocky bastions separated by channels.

B - The rocks of the northeast shallow are covered with a thin layer of algae, due to the effects of hydrodynamics and the work of grazing fish and invertebrates.

C - The base of the rocks is often colonized by yellow gorgonians and orange sponges, a sign that the sea carries in nutrition to these invertebrates even near the sea floor.

D - The Molarotto landscape is distinguished by the presence of rocky projections rising up vertically.

E - The water at Molarotto is always crystal clear, and abundant light penetrates, making the scene even more fascinating.

F - Morays, sometimes in groups of two or three in the same lair, are common among the masses on the seabed. They can often be seen even during the day as they slither out in the open among the rocks.

G - The upper portions of the shallow are always surrounded by a dense cloud of damselfish.

H - Large red scorpionfish are common on the deeper rocks of the shallow.

G - A blenny hovers among the algae that cover the shallower rocks. Blennies prey on small invertebrates, which they capture with swift movements; in fact, their bodies are designed to dart forward rapidly and not to swim long distances.

dive. As you swim among the masses, morays seem to be everywhere: large specimens peep out of almost every fissure, sometimes two or three of them at once. It is not uncommon to see them swimming quite far from the rocks, ready to take cover if divers approach. You will also see large red scorpionfish which are not easy to spot due to their remarkable mimetic abilities. The rock bastions toward the open sea terminate almost vertically, forming walls which on their northern sides are covered with red sponges and golden zoanthids. Like the granite of the emerging reef, underwater as well the rocks are furrowed by deep fissures, *tafoni* and passage holes,

E

and create quite a lovely scene. In the fissures hide large groupers which can often be seen out in the open, head down. The shallow has special attractions. You may see an enormous ray, sometimes poised on the patches of detritus on the seabed and sometimes on a flat rock. The summer spectacle is a large school of Mediterranean barracudas patrolling the shallow. But above all, as you swim upward on the return trip, it is possible to see large pelagic fish, including amberjacks, dentex, and even swordfish. Yet one of the most beautiful spectacles on this shallow, as you ascend, is the enormous cloud of damselfish that rhythmically drifts above the spires of the rocks illuminated by the sun.

F

G

H

I

THE WRECK OF MOLARA

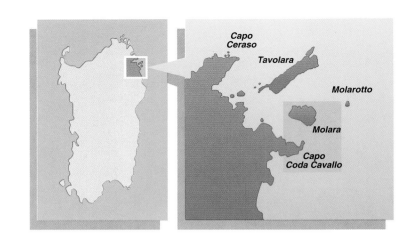

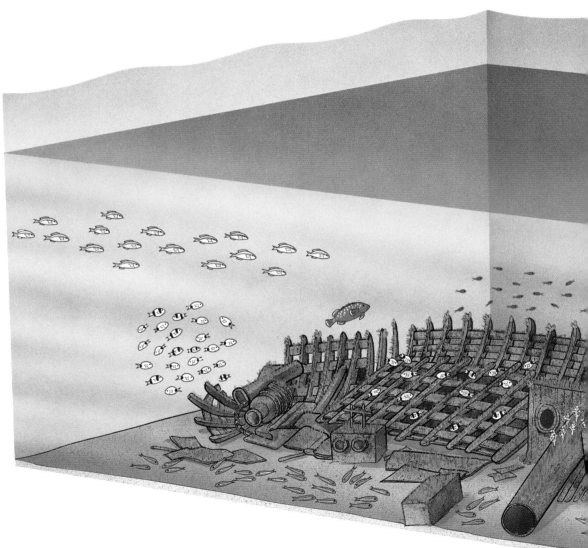

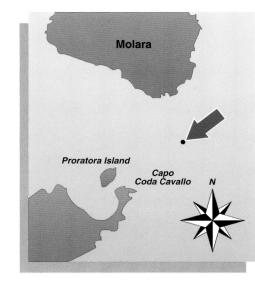

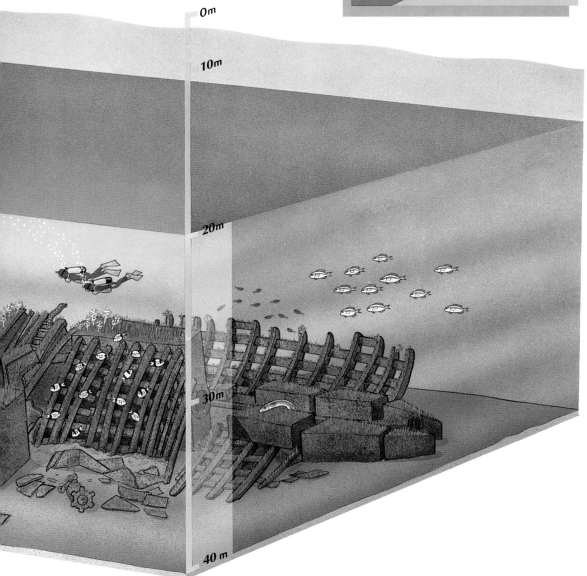

Between Molara and Capo Coda Cavallo on a sandy seabed 39 meters deep lies the large hulk of a wreck which until recently was largely still a mystery. For a long time it was thought to be an armed cargo ship transporting provisions that was torpedoed by a British submarine, as was the case of many other wrecks along the Sardinian coast. There are witnesses to such an event who recount how the ship caught fire before sinking. Yet many clues seem to indicate that the ship referred to in these tales was another one that appears to be lying on the sea floor not far from the Molara wreck. This ship is indeed quite damaged and shows clear signs of a fire. Not only does the Molara wreck show no sign of fire, but above all the type of construction and the age of the ship seem to place it well before 1943. Recent research and a new eyewitness to the events now give us a rather clear picture of what happened during the early months of 1943. Outside of Capo Coda Cavallo in the early spring of that year,

C

D

B - The wreck of Molara was a three-mast ship built in the second half of the 19th century. The photo shows the support of the stern mast, which is lying in the sand on the left side of the wreck.

C - The wreck had few structures on the deck: in addition to the masts in the stern area there were the smokestacks, which have now been destroyed.

D - The ship was a mixed iron and wood construction. Only a few fragments remain of the wooden portions, while the iron frame is well-preserved. Many organisms, especially lilac sponges (Haliclona mediterranea), have colonized the higher structures.

A

B
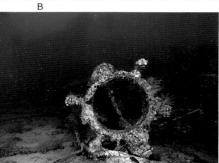

A - During World War Two the Italian and German convoys that sailed along the eastern coast of Sardinia were subject to continuous, damaging attacks by English submarines. In 1943, two ships were sunk not far from Capo Coda Cavallo: a minesweeper and the Molara wreck.

English submarines sank at least two ships, a mine-sweeper and old, creaky steamboat which was transporting bales of tobacco and probably grain. While the first has not yet been found, it is probably the "armed cargo ship" of which there has been so much talk, while the second is probably our wreck. It is a large ship of mixed wood and steel construction, over 70 meters long and in all likelihood with a gross tonnage of over 2,000. It was a motor sailer, or a ship with mixed propulsion, both sail and steam - this is quite clear from the great two-piston steam engine and the support structures of the two masts clearly visible on the wreck.

These two clues decisively date the construction of the ship to the end of the 19th century, placing it in that brief transitory phase in the history of naval construction that led to the disappearance of large sailing ships and the definitive victory of motor navigation, which was safer and faster. When it was sunk it was already almost an antique. Probably of French origin, it was headed for Marseilles from Syria. In addition to its French captain, it had a crew of 12-13 black seamen. It was torpedoed in the open sea by a British submarine. Only its captain was captured, while its crew, which had taken refuge on a lifeboat, was released. With this explanation of its history and the reason for its sinking, the Molara wreck is above all a piece of industrial archeology of great historical interest that adds further charm to the dive. Enter the water, and at a depth of about 20 meters the dark shape of the wreck begins to materialize on the faint light of the seabed. The highest portions at a depth of 35 meters consist of the large section that contained the enormous steam engine, the smokebox and the boiler. The smokestack has fallen toward the left side and the end is resting on the sand. The ship appears dismembered, and it takes some time to determine the position of the hull and identify the various pieces piled on top of each other, because little remains of the planking and the other wooden coverings. Along the steel frames around the joint nails only a few fragments of wood remain, which have resisted only because they are permeated with iron oxide. The double T-shaped large beam of the keelson which, given its position, shows that the hull is resting on its left side and that the right side has collapsed, falling on top of it, is clearly visible. Given the depth, it is not possible to visit the whole wreck in a single dive, and thus you should concentrate on the aft side and the steam engine. From the engine area move to the right side of the hull where the structures of the frame poke out from the sand, looking like the rib cage of a large whale. The ends of the frame are covered by violet-colored tubular sponges that stand out in your flashlight beam on the rusted iron. Moving toward the stern, you will come to the end of the large transmission shaft with its various flange joints. Around the axle are scattered tank caissons, formed to fit the hull as it narrowed. There is no trace of the propeller. Coming back toward the engine, the tangle of structures becomes chaotic. The upper part of the right side has collapsed on the left, and in the

F

G

E - The iron beam of the keelson runs through the central portion of the hull. On it are the flanges that supported the bearings of the propeller axle.

F - The steam engine is lying on its side, and among the pipes and iron fragments there are several gauges which have lost their glass faces, but not their pointers.

G - The motor had two cylinders and three columns. The enormous attachment flange of the propeller axle is clearly visible.

H - Schools of seabreams, numerous morays, conger eels and large groupers hide among the remains of the hull.

E

H

middle swim numerous two-banded seabreams, many of which are enormous for this species. You then come to the engine. It is a double effect steam engine with two cylinders and three support columns. The connecting flange of the axle and a group of gauges that still have their pointers are quite visible on the motor. Enormous seabreams also swim inside the engine. Among the

scrap iron hide a large moray and big groupers, which are quite timid even though they often hide just below the tallest pieces of wreckage. Colonies of hydrozoans grow on the higher portions, often grazed by brightly colored nudibranch gastropods (*Flabellina ischitana*), while tall fronds of sargassum are supported by aerocysts. Under the engine is a pile of bricks

which made up the refractory covering of the boiler, which is right under the large smokestacks. Until recently a conger eel known as Willie lived here. Accustomed to divers, Willie would rub up against them in exchange for a small fish. He is now gone, because someone with tanks dove all the way down here to shoot him, an act which was as stupid as it was illegal. The mouths of the smokestacks have been colonized by brightly colored sea anemones that take advantage of the channeling effect of the currents passing through the large tubes. This classical wreck dive ends here, and as you ascend you will see piles of materials along the left side: caissons, cables and various fragments. You can see the two windlasses near the bow, which has split open like a walnut, with a nice school of seabreams swimming over it. Often, at the limits of visibility, you may see large dentex sailing by, and thus, as you rise to the surface, your sensation of having only glimpsed the secret of this wreck is compounded by the mysterious fascination of the great pelagic fish.

SECCA DI OSALLA

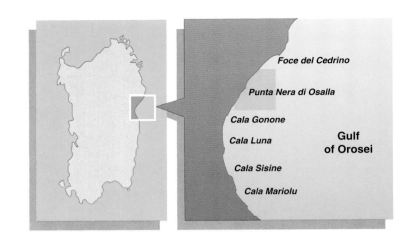

Foce del Cedrino
Punta Nera di Osalla
Cala Gonone
Cala Luna
Cala Sisine
Cala Mariolu

Gulf of Orosei

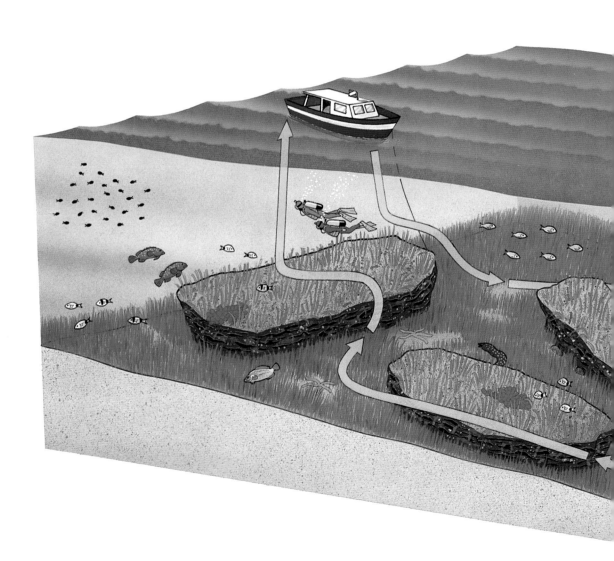

Punta Nera di Osalla

Cala Gonone

N

0m

10m

20m

24m

A

A - Secca di Osalla is a vast area in which meadows of Neptune grass alternate with rocky surfaces. The rocks often form channels with vertical walls colonized by colorful invertebrates.

B - The flashlight beam shining on the shadowy rocks reveals yellow, orange and blue sponges and many other invertebrates. The contrast with illuminated areas, where Neptune grass predominates, is quite evident.

*C - The floor of the shallow is quite varied: it goes from one rocky area to another, and each crevice reserves surprises and interesting sights.
A good flashlight is always useful for illuminating dark crevices.*

D - Pink patches of red calcareous algae, large orange patches of encrusting sponges and the colors of many other invertebrates stand out at the base of the rocks.

On the boundary between the coast of Dorgali and that of Orosei, the beach at Osalla is divided in two by a basalt promontory. Located a half mile out to sea, Secca di Osalla is a broad plateau with a summit 14 meters deep that terminates on the sandy seabed at a depth of 24 meters. The shallow is covered by a luxuriant meadow of Neptune grass from which emerge areas of basalt rock. Neptune grass also grows on the summit of the rocks, which are surrounded by gullies and areas of detrital erosion. The environment only appears to be monotonous, while in reality the sparse rocks make it quite varied and intriguing, as it is full of dens in the transition

B

C

D

E

zones between the Neptune grass and the wide precoralligenous and coralligenous areas that cover, respectively, the highest and lowest areas of the masses. Wandering among the rocks and following the channels which often form, you will soon note the richness of the area. Wrasses, pickerels and large black seabreams swim about and there is a grouper around every mass. Many morays peep out from the crevices in the coral, and it is often possible to see them in movement as well. Among the rhizomes of the Neptune grass you may see specimens of the uncommon *Chaetaster longipes*. In exposed areas, *Padina pavonica* and *Codium bursa* are common algae, while where the light wanes

E - The marc-colored laminae of the sea roses and the evanescent tufts of Acrosymphyton purpuriferum *grow abundantly in shadowy areas. The environment is also characterized by sea cactuses and other sciophilous organisms.*

F - Deerhorn corals (Pentapora fascialis) *form large masses; bryozoans are colonial animals and live within a skeleton, in this case in the form of calcareous laminae. The colony consists of thousands of small individuals.*

G - The rocks of the shallow are formed of basalt columns, similar to those seen on the coast. Sometimes Neptune grass colonizes even the summits of the shoals.

H - Triggerfish (Balistes carolinensis) *are fairly common on the reef. Although it is less colorful than its tropical cousins, the Mediterranean triggerfish has complex colors, with patterns in various shades of blue.*

I - A moray seems surprised by the light of the camera flash. Its spotted colors camouflage it, even when it is almost completely out in the open.

J - During the day, blotched pickerels form large groups near the surface of the water. At night they descend to the sea floor. By the light of the camera flash, their color, which from a distance appears uniform, reveals a complex pattern with shades of turquoise.

sea cactus (*Halimeda tuna*) predominates. On the walls of the large masses wide areas are covered by the pink scales of *Pseudolithophyllum expansum*, while on the less illuminated walls grow sea roses, algae typical of coralligenous areas. Large colonies of bryozoans (*Pentapora fascialis*) seem to form bushes that protrude out from the rock. The beauty of the dive lies in wandering from one rock to another, with the certainty of discovering something new at every turn. The contrast between the uniformity of the meadow, and the richness and variety of colors and organisms that cover primarily the lower parts of the rocks, is also quite interesting.

F

The dive should be approached with caution. Indeed, if you are not familiar with the area, it is not easy to orient yourself for the return. In addition, as you wander from mass to mass, you may be overtaken by the desire to keep going farther and extending your route. You also need to keep track of time, as you will be swimming at an average depth of 20 meters, and the minutes tick by quickly. There is one other aspect to consider: there is often a strong current on the shallow, and you must therefore absolutely avoid coming up too far from the anchor. You may find yourself emerging a great distance from the boat, with the obvious consequences.

G

H

I

J

THE KT OF OROSEI

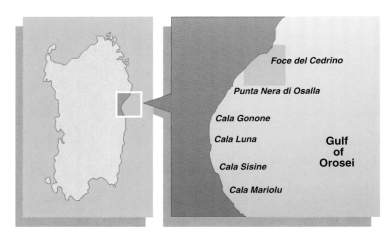

Foce del Cedrino

Punta Nera di Osalla

Cala Gonone

Cala Luna

Gulf of Orosei

Cala Sisine

Cala Mariolu

Foce
del Cedrino

N

Punta Nera di Osalla

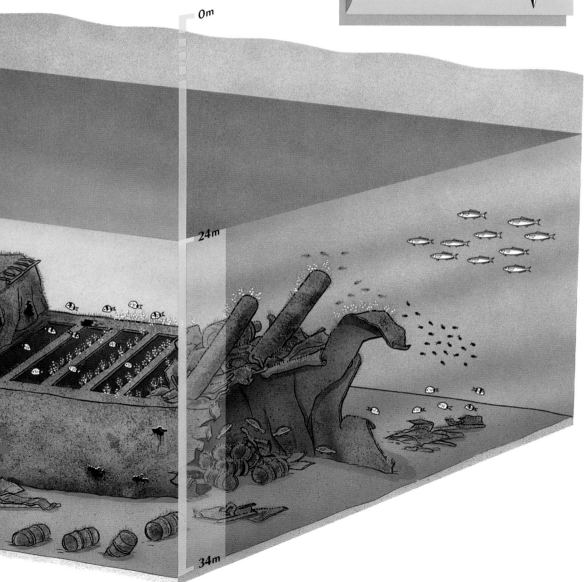

0m

24m

34m

A bout two miles offshore from Marina di Orosei, on a detrital seabed 34 meters deep, lies one of the most beautiful wrecks in the sea of Sardinia - the *KT*, a flat-bedded ship of German construction about 70 meters long.

This warship was equipped with a light gun in the stern area and at least four machine guns on the upper bridge and the bow cabin. It transported various self-propelled vehicles, including two cranes visible on the sea floor, various provisions and a large quantity of fuel and oil drums for the German troops stationed in Africa. It 1943 it was intercepted by the English submarine *Safari*,

A - The tall thalli of sargassum (Sargassum vulgare), a brown alga typical of areas with strong currents, grow on the parts of the wreckage closest to the surface. This alga is in fact quite common on the wreck and sometimes makes the dive difficult.

B - The supports for the lifeboats are still in place on the left side of the wreck. The cabin in the background was recently destroyed by the anchor of a passing cargo ship.

C - The skylight with the smokestacks and the air inlets for the engine room are located on the upper deck. In the background are two machine gun stands.

D - The light gun is near the stern on the upper deck. The ship was also armed with four heavy machine guns.

E - Only a few drums remain in the hold of the bow. The ship was carrying fuel, which was retrieved after the end of the war.

which also sank two other ships in the Gulf of Orosei.

It tried to elude the blockade, but was stopped by shots from the submarine that ripped through the bow and sank it.

Looking at it as it appears today, resting upright on the seabed, it appears that water entered the bow and the vessel sank quite rapidly without even time to abandon ship.

The wreck is well known not only to divers, for whom it has become almost a must, but also to the local inhabitants. Indeed, it is known as "the oil tanker."

For quite some time after it sank, fuel tanks bobbed to the surface and were recovered, while those

remaining in the hull and anything else that could be of some use were also removed.

An endless array of souvenirs is scattered throughout the houses of gulf inhabitants.

Although the dive is not deep, it is nevertheless difficult, as there is always a current, which is sometimes quite powerful, especially in the first few meters of the descent.

Usually the stern of the ship, the most intact portion, is the first thing to come into view.

The two propellers are in position at a depth of 34 meters, while up on the after deck, hatches and a structure, perhaps used to drag other boats, are visible.

F

F - Two automatic cranes are lying on the seabed to the right of the hull; a fragment of net entangled in the wreckage is lifted by the floats.

G - The large windlasses and hoist supports for lifting the front hatch are clearly visible in the bow area: the KT was a large landing craft with a bow that could be opened.

H - The stern is square, and a structure can be seen on the deck that was probably utilized to pull other boats.

I - The guardrail on the main deck has been completely colonized by a layer of algae and sponges. In the background the second deck is surmounted by the cannon.

E

G

On the wall of the cabins on the first deck you can see the rudder and the sheet anchor still in position.

On the second deck, pointing skyward, is a light gun mounted on a turret. Farther on there are two machine gun posts, with one of the two guns detached and lying on the deck, while the other is missing. Continuing toward the bow, you will see the skylight with the hatches of the engine room and two smokestacks, while on the left side the lifeboat supports are still in place. I came back to the *KT* for the first time in almost two years, and the beautiful command cabin which constituted the upper part of the

H

I

ship, surrounded by the guardrail and thrown over the forehold, has disappeared. Recently it was demolished, literally razed to the ground, by the anchor chain of a large cargo ship crossing along its left broadside.

Before what remains of the command cabin there are the black openings of the first forehold. Four large side-members traverse the entire width of the hull and form five big hatches from which one can descend down to the cargo level. Again toward the bow, there is a mass of wreckage within which can be seen a large windlass and two big pipes: in all probability they were the supports of the

B

A

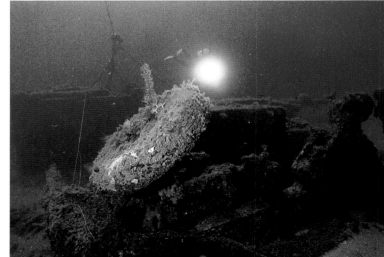

C

A - The rudder is on the eastern side of the cabins that supported the upper deck: all parts of the wreck have been covered by a thick layer of organisms.

B - The stern cannon, which has been completely encrusted, is mounted on a revolving turret. The handwheel for regulating its elevation is located on the left side.

C - The tires of the automatic equipment, located to the right of the ship, are covered with delicate violet-colored sponges and tall sargassum.

D - The wreckage of the bow is twisted and shattered, the result of the jolt and explosion of the torpedo that sank the ship.

D

E - The great hold of the bow was loaded with fuel drums: only those torn apart and punctured still remain on the seabed today. After the end of the war most of the ship's cargo was removed from the hold and the fuel was used by the local inhabitants.

F - The interior of the hold can be visited if you use great care and special techniques. Almost anything can be found among the rusty wreckage, including portions of the cargo and ship utensils.

G - The stairs connecting the decks and the holds are still in good condition. A thick layer of rust covers all metal structures. Only experienced divers with special training should enter the wreck.

H - The cabins on the main deck have lost almost all their walls, and the support beams are all that remain. Despite the depth, light filters even into the interior, creating lovely views.

I - The guide illuminates a group of gauges near the engine room. The internal portions of the hull are covered with a thin sediment which can rapidly cloud the water if stirred up.

capstans that made it possible to open the bow of the landing craft. In this area the sargassum grows to 50 centimeters high.

The bow is practically demolished: the two sides end in contorted wreckage, and that on the left is particularly spectacular.

From here descend to the seabed, which never exceeds a depth of 32.5 meters, where you will find the remnants of the load of drums that must have filled the hold. Those which remain have now broken up, and around them circles a good-sized school of brown meagres. You can turn back, passing through the forehold, which is completely empty, and then go back up

F

G

H

E

through one of the great passages on the deck and re-enter through the right broadside. In the cabins on the first deck swim quite large sharpsnout seabreams, while the whole area around the wreck is full of anthias. Not far from the hull along the broadside there are scattered piles of shattered fuel drums and the two large automated cranes, with their tires still intact.

Sometimes, swimming near the surface above the wreckage, you may find yourself surrounded by a schools of beautiful amberjacks, perhaps attracted by the bubbles of your tanks. It is a fitting end to a marvelous dive that never fails to reveals new secrets.

I

LA GALLERIA

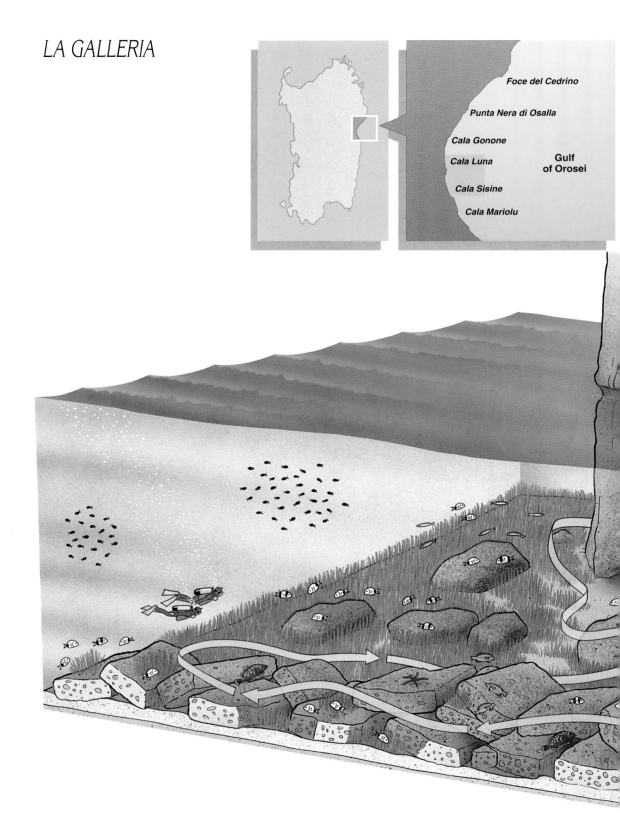

Foce del Cedrino

Punta Nera di Osalla

Cala Gonone

Cala Luna

Cala Sisine

Cala Mariolu

Gulf of Orosei

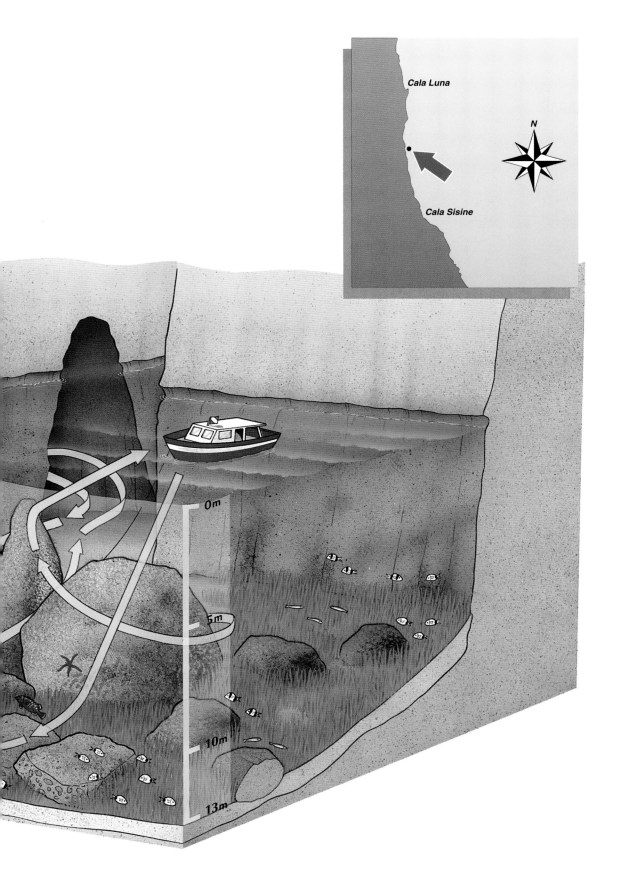

Cala Luna

N

Cala Sisine

0m

5m

10m

13m

The coast of the Gulf of Orosei is an extraordinary wall of limestone, furrowed by deep gorges and codule, or dried-out riverbeds. Especially near the surface of the sea, it is perforated by an endless array of caves, tunnels and cracks. Many of these cavities have an above-ground portion that continues underwater. Between Cala Luna and Cala Sisine, two stupendous beaches at the end of the codule of the same name, you can experience a dive that provides a synthesis of the seascapes along the entire gulf. The area is called Galleria because one of the two cavities you encounter during the dive runs across a projection of the wall from one side to the other. Moor the boat over a seabed about 13 meters deep scattered with calcareous masses that alternate with areas of white sand and

C

D

A - The long face of calcareous walls of the Gulf of Orosei is punctuated by thousands of cavities, both in and out of the water. Many underwater caves are easy to visit, offering beautiful seascapes in water just a few meters deep.

B - One of the many signs of passing time that distinguishes the coast of the gulf is the sequence of conglomerate blocks that faces La Galleria. This is the remains of a fossil beach, now colonized by algae and traversed by the long arms of starfish.

C - The great blocks resting on the sandy seabed form a group of crevices and passageways, where you can use your flashlight in an enjoyable search for fish and invertebrates.

D - The shallow depth and the clear water permit the entry of lovely shafts of light. The background offers a glimpse of the wall with the little cave passing through.

A

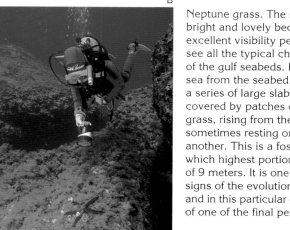
B

Neptune grass. The scenario is quite bright and lovely because the excellent visibility permits you to see all the typical characteristics of the gulf seabeds. Heading out to sea from the seabed, you will find a series of large slabs, partially covered by patches of Neptune grass, rising from the seabed and sometimes resting one on top of another. This is a fossil beach, which highest portion is at a depth of 9 meters. It is one of the many signs of the evolution of the coast, and in this particular case is evidence of one of the final periods of stable

sea level during the rise of about 120 meters that has brought the sea to its current level over the past 20,000 years. Observed from above, these blocks of conglomerates look almost like pavement, and in many areas they are so regular that they seem artificial. Brown meagres, seabreams and a few small groupers find refuge under the slabs, along with a large quantity of sessile organisms that live in dim light. The dive proceeds as you return toward the coast, where you will find large masses which have fallen from the wall, with sea urchins

E - The blocks of the fossil beach are so square and regular that they almost seem man-made.

F - The cave of La Galleria is an easy-to-explore tunnel that enters the limestone wall. The sandy seabed is traversed by ripple marks that indicate a fair amount of hydrodynamics.

grazing on the thin, felt-like layer of algae and large purple-colored red stars (*Ophidiaster ophidianus*) crawling by. At the foot of the wall is the first cave: its fine white sand floor at a depth of 7 meters and the waves that pass through it indicate significant hydrodynamics.

Just looking out from the opening provides a noteworthy sight: the turquoise blue of the entrance fades toward the interior, with quite beautiful lighting effects. The cave continues, turning to the left, and, with the entrance still in sight, you

H

E

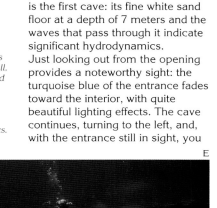

I

F

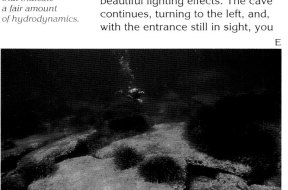

G

can ascend to a vault where an air bubble allows you to observe beautiful concretions. Another few meters ahead on the left the salt water mixes with fresh water flowing out, creating a strange mirror effect. To the right a rock formation looks like a large tree with big branches. Use your flashlight as you circle around the central column to return toward the entrance. Not only is the cave lovely, but on the walls there are sponges and annelids, while in the crevices hide large squills and swarms of shrimp. In the deeper tunnels your flashlight beam will reveal the long white antennae of banded shrimp (*Stenopus spinosus*). Leaving the cave, turn to the right along the wall and after a series of rocky masses enter the tunnel: the brief passage opens out on the other side of the rocky projection and has a vault covered with golden zoanthids. The return to the boat is accompanied by large masses: ascend along one of them that forms a pointed spire five meters below the surface, and after the safety stop reemerge with the boat just a few meters away.

G - The cuttlefish is quite common among the algae on the seabed. Its ability to rapidly change colors makes it quite mimetic, a skill useful for defensive purposes and hunting.

H - Octopuses are also common among the rocks on the seabed, where they often move about in search of prey. By using jet propulsion, the octopus can make rapid darts.

I - The white blenny (Blennius rouxi) is a small blenny that usually lives in holes or tubes anchored to the rocks, from which only its head emerges. Sometimes it abandons its refuge to hunt for small invertebrates.

THE WRECK
OF CALA LUNA

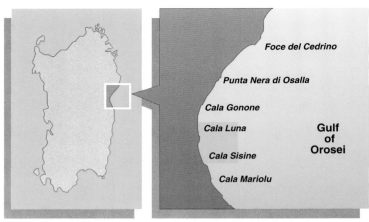

Foce del Cedrino

Punta Nera di Osalla

Cala Gonone

Cala Luna

Cala Sisine

Cala Mariolu

**Gulf
of
Orosei**

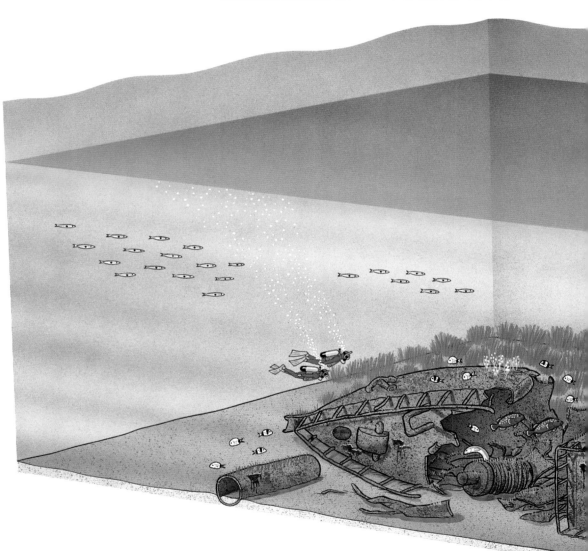

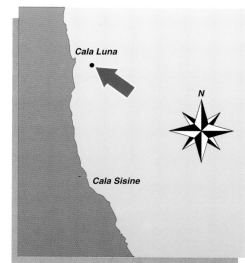

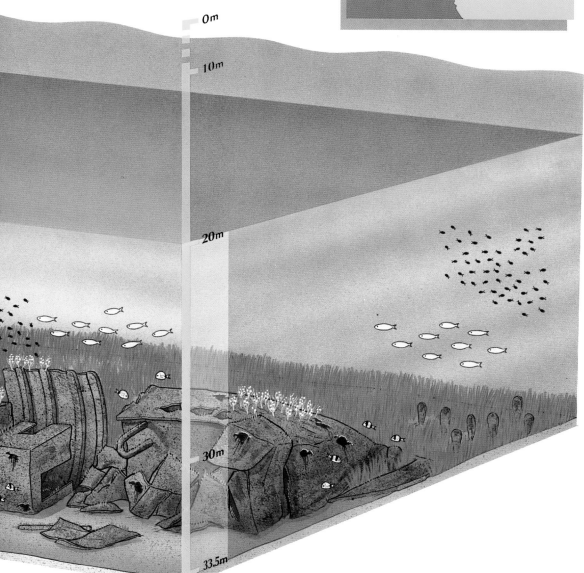

A - Cala Luna

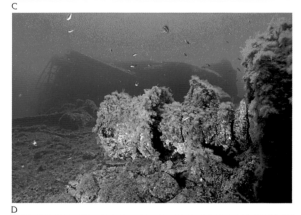

cross from Cala Luna, about a half a mile out to sea on a mixed seabed of detritus and Neptune grass, lies the wreck of the *Nasello*.
Built in Hamburg in 1921, it was an auxiliary, type F67 ship, and on April 3, 1943 it was transporting munitions for German troops.
Like the *KT* in the Gulf of Orosei, the Nasello was also hit by artillery from the Allied submarine Safari as it sailed across from Cala Gonone.
On that same day, the deadly British submarine, which in 1943 was patrolling the eastern coast of Sardinia, also sank the S. Francesco di Paola,

E

A - Cala Luna has become one of the classic summer holiday areas in Sardinia. Few know that on a fateful morning in 1943, two ships were sunk off this beautiful beach by the English submarine the Safari.

B - The bow of the Nasello *is resting on its left side: the ship was shattered by explosions and has shattered into three pieces. A fairlead on the front of the bow was probably used to pull the ship.*

C - A large windlass is clearly visible among the deck structures, with its steel cable still wound around the central coil.

D - The ship sank after it was hit by a torpedo that exploded the cargo of explosives it was transporting. Many structures were ripped out and lie piled on top of each other.

a 77 ton motor sailer, across from nearby Cala Sisine.
The *Nasello*, its center ripped by grenades, went adrift in the gulf before exploding and sinking.
The wreck, which was originally 42 meters long and 7.5 meters wide, is resting on its left side, and the devastated central area is standing up on end, unlike the stern and aft.
When you come to the stern, you will immediately see the large rudder lying on the seabed, and only one blade of the propeller sticks out of the sand.
Swim above the right broadside toward the deck, part of which is pulled out and reduced to contorted wreckage.

F

G - The small cabin in the center of the wreck is lying on its left side, while the upper portion is surrounded by a guardrail. All around there are piles of wreckage which are hard to identify.

H - Schools of seabreams and a pair of groupers can often be seen around the central portion of the wreck. One of the two groupers is extremely large.

I - In the stern, the rudder is lying on the sand, while one blade of the propeller is poking out of the sediment. Even at this depth the currents carry in sand and have slowly covered several structures.

Proceed along what remains of the deck structures toward the bow, and you will come to two rooms on the left side.

The first is smaller and its walls are mostly missing, while the larger second one must have been the higher part of the ship, with a guardrail along its upper perimeter.

The central area is a mass of wreckage which is not easy to identify. You can clearly see a large windlass with its steel cable still wound.

At least a portion of the right broadside seems to be standing. Here in the tangle of cables, iron slabs, pipes and plate live a pair of groupers.

One, a female, is small, while the other is a large male which weighs at least 20 kilograms. Sargassum grows on the raised portions; it is easily identifiable by its erect posture and the spherical cysts that grow at the base of the lance-shaped fronds.

The bow is at the end of the area hit by the explosion.

Lying on its left side, it seems practically intact: a guardrail follows its profile and on the small deck portion remaining there are several hatches, from one of which peeps the head of a beautiful conger eel.

At the end of the bow an anchor winch pulley is still in place, and the two anchors poke out of the hawseholes.

These are two Hall anchors weighing about 200 kilos each: the one on the left is clearly visible on the broadside, and as it is protruding it is kept clean by the current.

The one on the right is below the bow, but fully visible.

From the bow return toward the anchor, reaching a shallower depth in order to get a view of the entire hull.

When there is some current and visibility is good, an overall view of the hull not only gives you a better idea of the structure of the ship, but in particular shows you quite clearly the violence of the explosions that first ripped apart and then sank the *Nasello*.

G

H

E - The bow, still almost completely intact, is quite impressive. The anchors are still poking out of the hawseholes: the one on the right is clearly visible.

F - The right anchor, a Hall, has been kept clean by the currents. The left anchor can be seen under the bow.

I

THE SOUTHERN COAST: FROM ARBATAX TO BOSA

Capo di Monte Santu closes off the Gulf of Orosei from the south. This cape has a low outline with vegetation growing thickly down to the edge of the wall. Leave the vertiginous walls of the gulf behind you and descend south, passing the Pedra Longa spire where the calcareous landscape ends. From the little island of Ogliastra at the center of the Gulf of Tortolì to Capo Sferracavallo, the granite returns

Corona Niedda
Su Puntillone
S'Archittu
●ORISTANO
GULF OF ORISTANO
GULF OF ORO
Acituan Cav
Secca dell'Iso

Le Tacche Bianche
Scoglio del Corno
SAN PIETRO ISLAND
SAN ANTIOCO ISLAND
Banco Pomata
Scoglio del Toro

CAGLIARI
●
The Wreck of the Entella
The Wreck of the Romagna
Secca di Mez
GULF OF CAGLIARI

A

B

A - The small Oasis of Torre Seu in Sinis is a protected area managed by the WWF, and until La Maddalena Archipelago National Park was established it was the only coastal area of Sardinia which was protected.

B - The coast between Nebida and Masua is one of the wildest areas of the island. In the background to the left are the vertical walls of the Pan di Zucchero reef: the rocks on this stretch of the coast are the most ancient of the entire continent of Europe.

with jagged spires and pinnacles. Farther south on the coastal stretch at Salto di Quirra to Capo S.Lorenzo, the limestone returns. The whole area has very interesting seabeds with faboulous caves: unfortunately, it is subject to military restrictions. After Capo S.Lorenzo the stretch of coast from the mouth of the Flumendosa to Capo Ferrato, south of Muravera, is low and delimited by sandbanks with large marshes behind them, including the Colostrai marsh. Across from Capo Ferrato, again formed by volcanic rock, is a beautiful shallow which is also known as Secca delle Cicale due to the large quantity of these crustaceans that gather among the rocks in late spring. During World War II at least two large cargo ships were sunk here, although they lie at practically inaccessible depths. A little farther south the granite coast of Villasimius begins, with the islands of Serpentara and Cavoli off the coast. Unfortunately the entire stretch of sea from Serpentara to Capo Boi is restricted to archeological excavations, and diving is forbidden. Only recently have a few diving centers obtained permission to dive in certain areas. This is one of the most interesting areas in Sardinia for diving, yet a short-sighted desire to protect archeological treasures has prevented its use. Moreover, the prohibition has in no way stopped

poachers, and the illegal removal of archeological finds continues despite prohibitions. Fortunately, beautiful dives are possible even outside the area, on the offshore shallows and on the wreck of the Egle, a cargo ship lying 36 meters deep which was sunk by a submarine. The wrecks are one of the characteristic features of the seabeds in the Gulf of Cagliari: there are at least fifteen of them, but only two can be explored without diving over 40 meters deep. Across from the promontory of Torre delle Stelle, in addition to the remains of the *Entella*, the remains of two other convoy ships sunk between April 10 and 11, 1943 lie at depths between 40 and 70 meters. The *Loredan*, a 1,350 ton ship, lies in the deepest water, and in addition to still having cannons and machine gun posts in place, its wreckage is covered with large fans of red and yellow gorgonians. Passing the Gulf of Cagliari, there is yet another wreck just before Capo Teulada, where the hull of the *Dino*, a mercantile ship that was transporting clay and sank in 1973 during a sea storm, lies in the harbor of Porto Zafferano at a depth of 25 meters. Unfortunately, the wreck lies within the prohibited military zone, and in fact near Capo Teulada is a military exercise area and firing ground for the Decimomannu air base. In theory, it is prohibited to dive here as well, but on Sunday and during the summer the military makes an exception, and a few quick dives onto the wreck are possible - the usual Italian-style solution. Doubling the ancient calcareous cliffs of Capo Teulada, the islets of Toro, Vacca and Vitello prepare you for the two islands of S. Antioco and Carloforte. The outer edges of both islands offer wild landscapes almost untouched by humans. Underwater, there are numerous beautiful diving areas, where the most interesting aspect is offered by the clear difference in animal and plant groups that populate the submerged rocks. Compared with the northern and eastern coasts, you will immediately notice the difference in the algae coverage, the almost total absence of gorgonians and, for example, the greater number of ornate wrasses rather than rainbow wrasses: the exact contrary from the opposite coast. From the reef of Carloforte, which consists of dramatic masses of volcanic rock, look east to see the calcareous coast of the larger island. This is one of the zones with which divers are less familiar, for reasons which include the fact that tourism, with its joys and pains, has only just begun here, but it is also the oldest stretch of coast on the entire continent of Europe. Between Nebida and Masua the limestone, which in many areas drops sheer to the sea, is over 500 million years old. Across from the larger island is Pan del Zucchero, a steep calcareous rock covered with low vegetation only on its highest part. Underwater along its walls the seabed does not reach great depths, and interesting cavities open up in the calcareous rock. The coast continues high until the deep inlet of Cala Domestica. Then, passing Buggerru, the great beach of Portixeddu leads north to Capo Pecora. This is the wildest part of the coast on the island, mostly inaccessible by land and still unexplored by divers. And here the sea, exposed as it is to the west, is no laughing matter. One must go much farther north, to the Oristano area, to find organized diving centers. But before arriving, you will see extraordinary coastal

landscapes like the great dune area of Foci del Rio Piscinas. Active dunes of gold-colored sand penetrate about three kilometers inland, blown by westerly winds, while junipers and tenacious pioneer vegetation futilely try to halt the advancing sand. Farther north, the long peninsula of Capo Frasca closes off the end of the Gulf of Oristano. Here on the military firing range F104's flash by, and it is said that at least one lies on the floor of the Gulf of Oristano, a coveted wreck yet to be discovered. Capo San Marco with its ruins of Tharros projects out from Sinis to close off the gulf. The peninsula of Sinis is an extraordinary environment: the inland area is a succession of low hills and large marshes, which particularly in spring offer unforgettable images. The eight thousand flamingos of Sal'e Porcus, a pink streak on the diaphanous waters of the marsh in the red light of sunset, are a spectacle that is alone worth the entire trip. The coast is a succession of calcareous cliffs and sandy beaches - but this is no common sand. Billions of small, measured

granules of quartzite embellish the beaches of Mari Ermi and Is Arutas. The reef of Catalano and the island of Mal di Ventre with its interesting, often wind-swept seabeds emerge off the mixed seabeds of rock, detritus and Neptune grass. Mal di Ventre is perhaps most well-known for its Roman ship sunk with a load of lead bars. Certainly the merchant who lost this precious cargo never imagined that two thousand years later his lead would make a great contribution to scientific research on the physics of matter. Indeed, two of those bars, which contain no radioactivity due to the long period they have remained underwater, were utilized in the laboratory of Gran Sasso in studies of atomic particles. Passing Capo Mannu, you begin another stretch of coast which is in large part intact and where several diving areas are becoming famous. One example is the reef of Su Puntillone, a steep pinnacle that carries another exotic touch of the Atlantic. Indeed, here you can observe sea tangles, a class of algae which is certainly not a common sight in the Mediterranean.

C

D

C - The islet of Ogliastra in the Gulf of Tortolì marks the transition from the limestone walls of the Gulf of Orosei to the granite of the southern coast.

D - A small white lighthouse overlooks the southern wall of Toro Island. The island marks the southernmost tip of Sardinia, and is only accessible when the weather is good.

ACITUAN CAVES

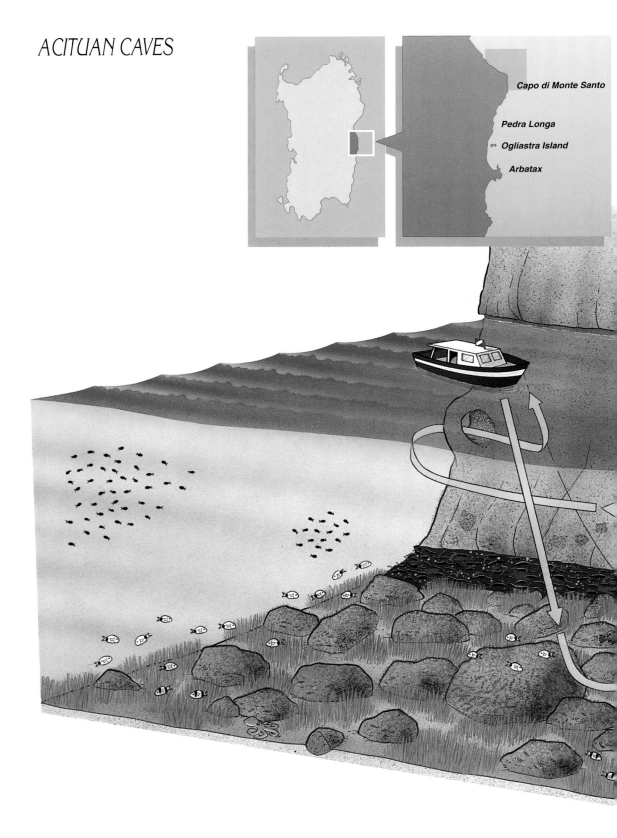

Capo di Monte Santo

Pedra Longa

Ogliastra Island

Arbatax

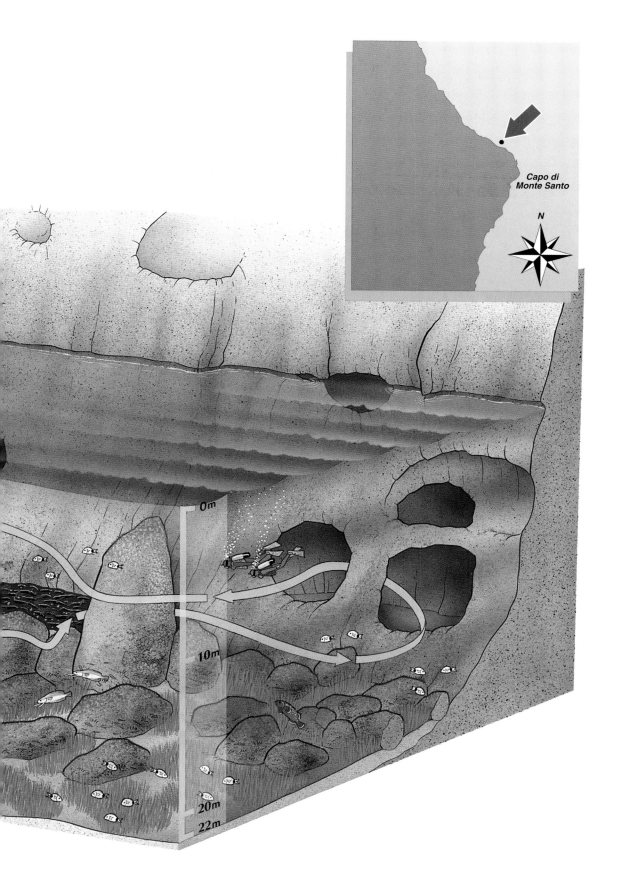

Capo di
Monte Santo

N

0m

10m

20m
22m

orth of Capo di Monte Santu a series of inlets breaks the continuity of the low cliff: first Portu Pedrosu, then Portu Quau, and finally Porto Iltiera. Immediately afterwards, the wall rapidly rises until it exceeds 200 meters in height, dropping sheer into the sea.

Moor your boat here on a seabed of mixed rock and sand about 22 meters deep.

The wall faces northeast, and the best hours for diving are in the early morning, because later the sun disappears and the whole diving area falls into shadow. In addition, when the sun is still low on the horizon it shines directly into the caves, creating

A

of shadow and light.

The interior of the cave is covered with typical organisms such as corals, sponges, bryozoans and polychaete worms. In late spring and early summer many squills gather in the cave for reproduction, and then return to deeper waters.

Turning left toward the crevice, you will immediately see the other two openings: the smallest is almost on the surface, while the other, which is perfectly circular, leads back to the wall at a depth of about 8 meters.

From here return to the boat, keeping the wall to your right: despite the shallow depth, due to the only brief periods of light this

B

C

D

beautiful plays of shadow and light. The dive begins on the deeper rock masses, where rather large white seabreams often can be seen. In the crevices forkbeards and small groupers can be seen, and in early summer you may encounter large octopuses.

In an environment characterized by red algae, ascend to a depth of 18 meters and come to a large oblong mass resting on the wall, with its base surrounded by smaller rocks.

The passage between the mass and the wall is carpeted by brightly colored sponges, retepora and other bryozoans.

Coming out of the small tunnel, skirt the wall where the many

species of sponges include acanthellae with their jagged forms. Sometimes in summer you may find a specialized predator on one of the sponges: known as *Phyllidia flava*, this golden nudibranch, uncommon in the Mediterranean, is a beautiful yellow color with raised white spots. A few meters farther on are the entrances to the caves, or rather the cave, because the four openings are connected.

The main entrance to the cavity is about 10 meters deep and is divided in two by a rock bridge. From the interior looking out the scene is quite lovely: the rays of the sun pass through the upper opening, creating beautiful plays

A - Due to the position of the wall, this area receives only a few hours of light daily, and the sun illuminates the entry of the caves only during the early morning. The wall is covered with sciophilous organisms and algae typical of areas with strong hydrodynamics.

B - The Gulf of Orosei is closed off to the south by Capo di Monte Santu. At the end of the gulf the walls become higher and plunge down into the depths, traversed by innumerable cavities.

C - The cavity has three connected entrances that form lovely plays of light and shadow when the sun is still low on the horizon.

D - The walls of the cave in the outer areas are covered with sponges, corals, bryozoans and annelids. Algae are completely absent due to lack of light.

E - The shallowest entrance is almost at the surface. The carpet of organisms on the walls grows increasingly sparse as you proceed into the cavity.

F - At the base of the cliff the flashlight beam illuminates red algae, numerous yellow sponges and green sea cactuses and sea fans.

G - A grouper seeks refuge in a cavity in the wall: in ambient lighting, the colors of this yellow-spotted fish are actually quite mimetic.

H - Red stars (Echinaster sepositus) are the most common species on the Sardinian seabeds.

is a classic precoralligenous environment. Here along the wall the seascape changes with the seasons. During the winter the brown algae degrade and the various species of red algae predominate.

In spring sunlight increases and the brown algae begin to grow again, especially *Dictyopteris*, which covers over the winter carpet. In late summer, on the upper areas of wall near the surface, the rock seems alive with the drifting fronds of brown algae that add movement to color. Your slow ascent to the surface will be an extremely entertaining exploration: crevices, holes and fissures alternate on the wall, and

E

F

G

H

inside you can observe an endless array of organisms. Predominating at depths of 5 meters to the surface are golden zoanthids, which stand out on the red of the sea roses and other algae. Almost at surface level, a little rock arch is carpeted with golden zoanthids and bryozoans, and often a small grouper seems to play hide-and-seek.

Emerge at the wall with the boat a few meters away. In late summer don't forget to look up - you will see one of the most extraordinary natural sights in the Mediterranean. In fact, this area is one of the few nesting places of the eleonora falcon, a rare and extremely elegant species.

SECCA DELL'ISOLOTTO

Capo di Monte Santo

Pedra Longa

Ogliastra Island

Arbatax

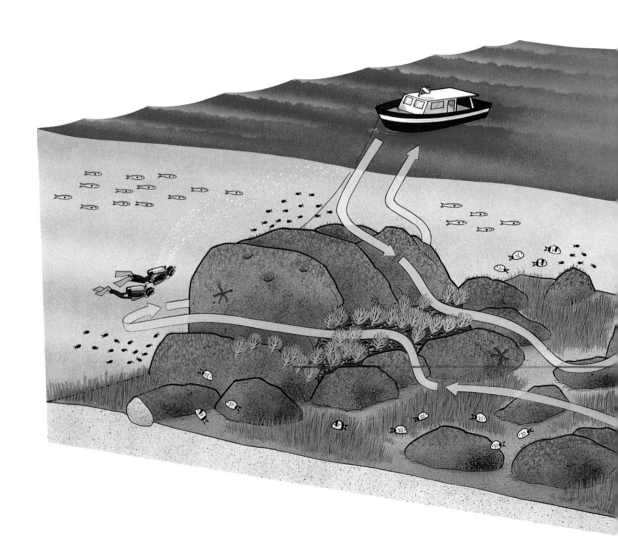

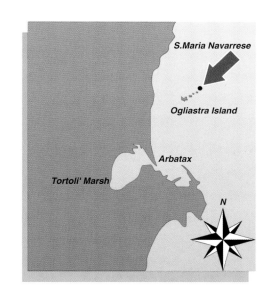

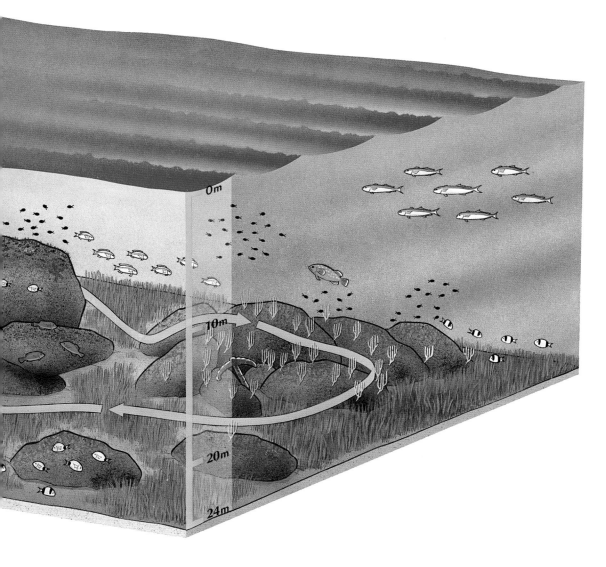

I n the center of the Gulf of Arbatax a series of rocky reefs forms the islet of Ogliastra. Only the largest reef is covered by low vegetation, while the others are a group of windswept granite pinnacles and towers lashed by the sea and covered with the guano of the seagulls and cormorants that nest here. North of the last rock, starting at a depth of 13 meters, is the Secca dell'Isolotto. Numerous emerging granite rocks rise from a seabed about 24 meters deep, covered by a luxuriant meadow of Neptune grass which is only occasionally interrupted by patches of sand. Moor on the highest rocks, and as you descend underwater, head east. The water

A

is almost always limpid, and the overall view is impressive.

Even the meadow of Neptune grass contributes to the beauty of the scene, as it fills the gullies between the rocks and almost seems to be a connecting element. The rocks are covered with a soft layer of algae from which numerous hydrozoans poke out. On the colonies of *cnidaria* several species of nudibranchs graze and reproduce, including *Cratena peregrina* and *Flabellina affinis*. The former deposits ribbons of white eggs, the latter violet. In the fissures of the rocky masses groupers, brown meagres and a few seabreams make their dens. Moving east, you will see more masses. Among these you will

B

C

D

E

easily spot the one that gives the shallow its name - a pointed, thin pinnacle that rises from the seabed slightly away from the other rocks. One side is covered with yellow gorgonians. Right in front of the largest rock is a brightly colored vault. Proceeding east, cross a stretch of Neptune grass and come to a group of smaller rocks on which a large anchor rests. At first sight it seems like a modern admiralty, but it is not. The lack of bills on the flukes, the evident presence of the crown and the condition of the concretions, all point to a much older piece of equipment. Looking ahead, you can make out more masses, and you are likely to see a large dentex or an amberjack. In the fissures among the rocks grow

A - One wall of this shallow, which takes its name from a rock which resembles a razor, is covered with yellow sea fans.

B - The seascape changes radically from the emerging rocks to those which cover the seabed off the islet of Ogliastra.

C - An anchor, perhaps from the period of imperial Rome, is lying in the central area of the shallow. All that remains of it today is the concretion formed by the oxidation of the original metal.

D - Neptune grass grows luxuriantly in the channels that divide the various emerged rocks covering the sea floor.

E - The tallest rocks on the shallow are exposed to the light and covered with a layer of algae.

F - White sea fans (Eunicella singularis) are quite common in the fissures between the rocks.

G - A colony of very large white sea fans grows on the edge of a rock.

H - A cardinal fish hovers in a crevice: this specimen is a male in the reproductive state. The swelling below the jaw is an indication that he is incubating the eggs the female has deposited in his mouth.

I, J - Alicia mirabilis, the most stinging anemone of the Mediterranean, has nocturnal habits. By day it is unrecognizable, as its tentacles are retracted, while at night they expand in search of food.

colonies of large white gorgonians, *Eunicella singularis*: they look somewhat more unkempt than the usual yellow gorgonians and are easily identifiable by their lighter, whitish color. From the anchor start your return toward the boat, passing by other groups of rocks. In the zones facing north at the base of the masses you will see concretions of red algae full of crevices and color. Big red stars (*Ophidiaster ophidianus*) crawl among the algae, while large, peaceful whitetip sea urchins (*Sphaerechinus granularis*) are busy grazing. The algae covering is often interrupted by folds and vaults in the rock colonized by colorful organisms, especially sponges and bryozoans. Under one

F

of these little vaults you are likely to spot a tiny white grouper that you can observe as it floats against the yellow background of the golden zoanthids. Come back to the first group of rocks from the south, where the granite descends vertically to the sea floor, then go around the masses and come back to the mooring line, from where you can ascend, surrounded by a cloud of damselfish. The Secca dell'Isolotto should also be explored at night in order to get a glimpse of one of its biggest stars, a splendid berried anemone (*Alicia mirabilis*), practically invisible on the largest rocks and distends its soft tentacles. This is the most beautiful and most stinging sea anemone in the Mediterranean, and it alone makes the dive worthwhile.

H

I

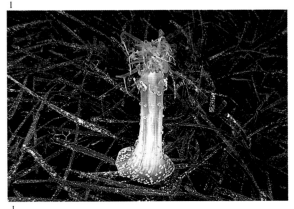

J

SECCA DI MEZZO

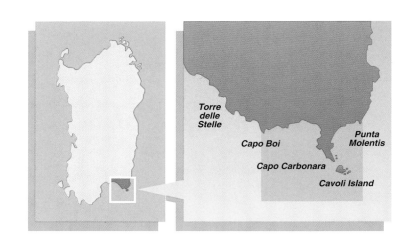

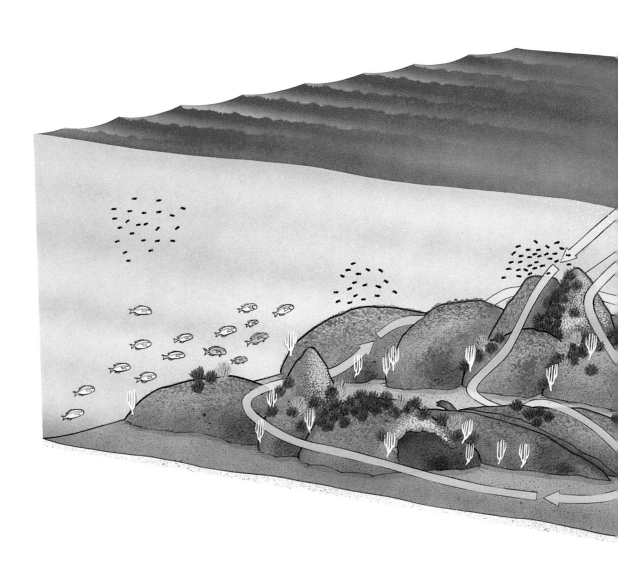

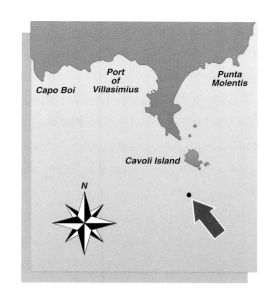

Cavoli Island is located at the far southeastern tip of Sardinia across from Capo Carbonara. The coast of the cape and the island are characterized by smooth grey granite full of holes carved by the processes of erosion. As in Gallura, the forms of the granite seem made to stimulate the imagination, and it is easy to make out bears, morays and human faces sculpted in the rock. Toward the south below sea level ridges of rock branch off to form rises at various depths offshore. About a mile from the island the Secca di Libeccio extends for some distance,

with its shallowest point at a depth of 15 meters. Another top reef is located at a depth of 24 meters and is called Secca di Mezzo because it is located between land and the highest point of the shallow. Fortunately, the whole area is outside the prohibited archeological area that runs from Capo Boi east of Capo Carbonara to Cala Pira on the eastern coast. This is a beautiful dive for experts, because it is in the deep sea at an average depth of 30 meters. Moor at the highest point of the shallow where two vertical masses are separated by a large cleft carpeted with golden zoanthids. The shallow has

B - The summit and the fissures among the granite masses that cover the floor are covered with large sea fans that stand out against the yellow of the golden zoanthids.

C - Many north-facing walls are covered with a carpet of quite large golden zoanthids (Parazoanthus axinellae).

A

C

B

D

a series of ridges located perpendicular to the coast, separated by tongues of sand and surrounded by scattered rocky masses. The ridges are full of transversal cracks, where the currents pass through. The first thing you will note is that the rocky area facing north and the clefts are carpeted with red gorgonians and golden zoanthids. After this first eye-catcher, turn east and cross a sandy channel to reach another rocky area, where under a large round mass a big lead anchor stock from a Roman anchor is lying 36 meters deep.

D - Sea fans rise from the rocks, which are literally covered with a layer of various species and colors of encrusting sponges.

E

Covered with red sponges, the anchor stock is slightly curved, and all around it are gorgonians and white sea fans (*Eunicella singularis*). Right under the anchor lives a beautiful moray, poking halfway out as it lies in wait of prey. Returning westward, cross a sandy clearing where another Roman anchor, or rather the concretion of an iron anchor probably dating from the imperial period, stands against the granite wall. Both the shaft and the flukes are broken, and you can clearly see the square iron section. Even when there are no prohibitions, the rule is: look but don't

E - The stock of a Roman anchor covered by encrusting sponges lies on the sea floor at the foot of the rocks. The square hole in which the wooden beam of the anchor was inserted is clearly visible in the center of this lead artifact.

H

touch. Returning to your starting point, you will see a beautiful wall full of red gorgonians: those located near the bottom are quite large. In addition to the sea fans, there are many yellow and white gorgonians, while the walls of the rocks are covered with large golden zoanthids, enormous colonies of bryozoans (*Pentapora*) and concentrations of *Filograna*, an annelid with thin white tubes. In the crevices are groupers, while in the illuminated areas ocellated wrasses swim. At the base of the shallow schools of large white seabreams can be seen. Explore this area, swimming at the depth of the rocks. Given the good visibility, the highest peak is always in sight, but there are no problems in orientation because the position of the rocks always makes it possible to determine where you are. The clear water and the large numbers of organisms on the reef are a clear indication that this is an area full of currents: often the surface current runs in a different direction from that on the sea floor, and this needs to be taken into consideration when planning the dive.

F

G

F - A moray peers out of a crevice surrounded by golden zoanthids and red and brick-colored algae.

G - The small locust lobster is similar to the larger locust lobster, but can easily be distinguished by both its size and its more colorful shell. The small locust lobster is primarily nocturnal.

H - A small crab (Inachus sp.) finds refuge at the base of the tentacles of a large anemone (Anemonia sulcata). Immune from the stinging cells of the anemone, the crab is safe from predators.

THE WRECK
OF THE ENTELLA

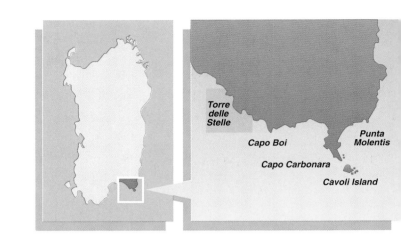

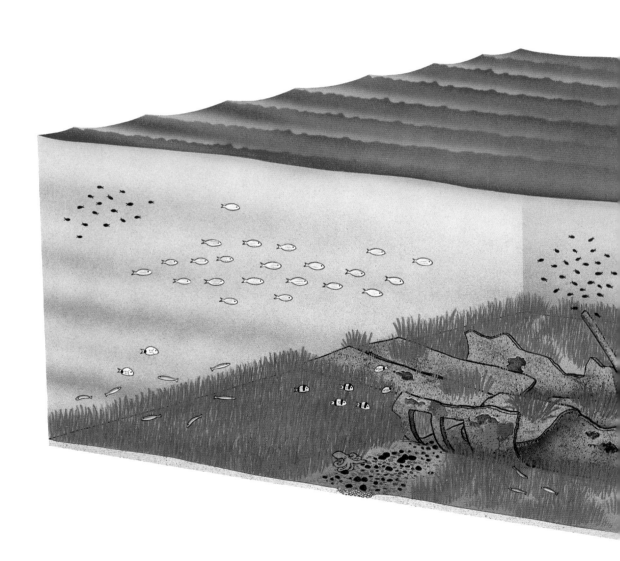

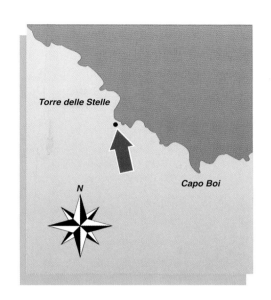

A few dozen meters from the cape of Torre delle Stelle, on a seabed that slopes down to a depth of 16 meters, lie the remains of the *Entella*, one of three convoy ships sunk in 1943 by the usual British submarine. The other two lie much deeper: the wreck of the *Isonzo* is at a depth of 42 meters, while the *Loredan* is over 50 meters deep. The captain of the *Entella*, unlike those of the two bigger ships, saw the trail of the torpedoes approaching, and to avoid the deadly assault literally turned the prow of the ship onto the reef of the cape.

He was thus able to avoid not only the explosion, but most importantly the rapid sinking that was the fate of the *Loredan* and the *Isonzo*. Run aground, the *Entella* was then bombarded, and it sank right at the foot of the rocks of the cape, where it was further destroyed with explosive charges, as it was a hazard for navigation.

The remains of the lower part of

C

D

A - Only fragments of the lower portion of the hull of the Entella remain. The supports of the axle bearings and other unidentifiable wreckage can be seen in the stern area.

B - The remains of the wreck have been colonized by innumerable organisms, so that what remains of the hull almost seems to have been swallowed up by the seabed.

C - Patches of Neptune grass growing next to the twisted wreckage seem to be engulfing the wreck.

D - The hull of the Entella was destroyed in stages. After foundering on the rocks, it sank and was then once again exploded apart.

A

B

the hull are resting on a detrital seabed, mixed with the shattered fragments of a load of coal the ship was transporting.

In the more sheltered areas of the wreckage there are still fragments of coal, and some say that if it were removed from the water it would still burn well.

Almost half of the hull is covered with luxuriant tufts of Neptune grass that hide the overall view, but at the same time integrate it extraordinarily well with the marine environment.

Neptune grass grows only on that portion of the hull, and among the long green leaves only a few fragments of the structure poke out: the form of the ship's bottom, which seems to surround the little meadow, is visible only if you move to the side of the wreck.

The stern portion is uncovered, although very little remains of it. In the center of the curve of the hull are the supports of the axle bearings, alongside which ran pipes and various cables.

E - The Neptune grass that grows on the sea floor near the bow area of the wreck has also colonized the wreckage.

F - The outer side of the bottom of the ship is covered by colorful invertebrates, and many species of fish have found shelter below the wreckage.

Very little can be made out: a few pipes turned upward are somewhat of a sight.
The highest is 9 meters deep, and all are covered with luxuriant colonies of hydrozoans where colorful nudibranchs often graze. *Cratena, Flabellina* and *Coryphelia*, which feed on the polyps of hydrozoans, are the most common genera.
Colonies of *cnidaria* are common in many other areas of the wreck, which due to its somewhat elevated position on the flat sea

H

E

I

F

G

floor is often swept by currents. In general, the wreck has become a refuge for a large variety of organisms, some of which are rather rare, such as the long-spined urchin (*Centrostephanus longispinus*) hidden under the right side of the ship bottom. You may also see a few echinoderms (*Antedon mediterranea*), and if you look carefully among its tentacles you may spot a tiny symbiotic shrimp, perfectly camouflaged. Octopuses and small groupers hide among the wreckage, wrasses make their nests there and numerous orange and blue sponges find surfaces to grow on.
This very quantity and variety of organisms scattered on the wreckage and the small but luxuriant meadow that covers a portion of the wreck are what makes this dive interesting, a sort of revenge for the tragedy that caused its sinking and the rending explosions that almost totally destroyed it.

G - Despite the shallow depth, a flashlight is indispensable in order to observe the organisms that live under the wreckage.

H - The hull of the Entella *offers innumerable shelters for various organisms. Many octopuses make their lairs among the wreckage, where they hunt at night.*

I - Sea lilies (Antedon mediterranea) can be seen among the wreckage of the ship and on the Neptune grass. These organisms usually live attached to a support through the cirri located on their undersides, but they can also swim, elegantly moving their long arms.

THE WRECK
OF THE ROMAGNA

Poetto

Porto
Armando

Port of Cagliari

Gulf of Cagliari

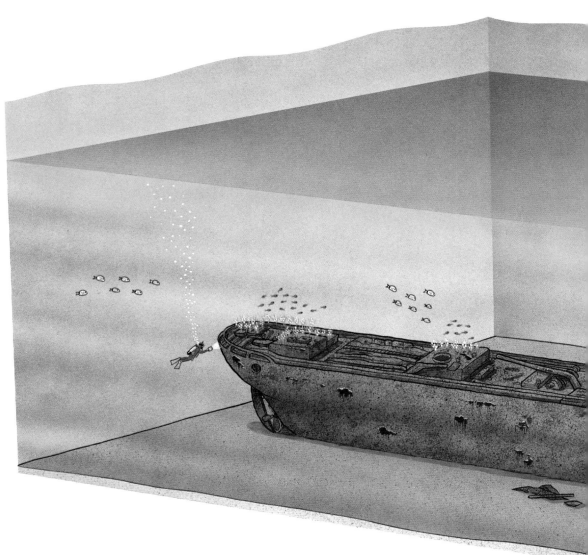

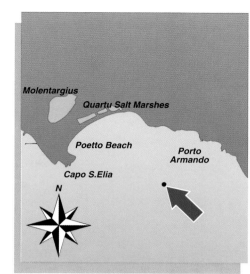

Molentargius

Quartu Salt Marshes

Poetto Beach

Porto
Armando

Capo S.Elia

N

0m

10m

20m

30m

40 m

43 m

A

B

The *Romagna* was an old 1416 ton tanker built in 1899 which was requisitioned by the Navy to Cagliari on October 4, 1941. On August 2, 1943 the oil tanker was transporting its precious cargo of fuel to Cagliari, where it was of strategic military importance, especially for the air force, which was engaged in defending the island.

The *Romagna* was escorted by six small antisubmarines and two pairs of Macchi 202 and 205. At eight o'clock in the morning, when it was only a few miles from the port of Cagliari, the *Romagna* plowed into a mine from a mine defense that had been recently placed and of which land positions

C

D

had probably not advised the tanker: since the beginning of the war, over 5,000 mines had been placed in minefields in the Gulf of Cagliari and along the Sardinian coast. The explosion of the device blew away the bow and caused the fuel to ignite. The ship, stopped in its tracks, then foundered out of control. The *Romagna*, completely devastated by the fire and the explosion of the fuel, sank about a kilometer away from the point where it ran into the mine.

Today it lies upright in the sand, about a hundred meters long, looking almost as if it were ready to sail again as it was when it was stopped by the mine that tore the bow from the rest of the ship.

Go down twenty meters along the mooring line in totally blue waters until the enormous form of the *Romagna* suddenly appears 15 meters farther below.

The highest sections are 32 meters deep. Almost everything has collapsed on the deck, including the great yards and the smokestacks, while only the lower parts of the cabins remain. Near the stern the wreckage seems held together by a myriad of nets and ropes: be very careful not to get entangled in them.

Leaning out of the hull, the sense of enormity increases.

Descend to the aft bottom, more than ten meters below, and the sight of the enormous propeller and the rudder alone makes the dive worthwhile. The blades are longer than a man and the rudder is 5 or 6 meters high. The view from below is truly spectacular. The wreck is enveloped in a cloud of anthias, while the sandy sea floor is a carpet of black bristlestars. Coming back to the deck, it is not easy to decipher the contorted wreckage and what it once was.

A good number of dives are necessary to get an overall view. Tall sargassum grass, some of it 50 centimeters high, grows on the wreckage, while every so often a school of large white seabreams passes by, and several good size scorpionfish lie in wait, motionless. Large conger eels and morays hide in the pipes and scrap.

A - The Romagna *is lying on a sandy seabed that in many areas is covered by a myriad of black bristlestars. These starfish, which at times are crowded around the same prey, provide a most unusual sight.*

B - The view of the imposing stern of the Romagna *may be the most impressive moment of the entire dive. A comparison with the size of the diver reveals its enormity.*

C - The rudder and the blade of the propeller are still in place. A photograph with a diver shows how enormous the blades of the ship actually are. The projecting curve of the transom can also be seen.

D - The Romagna *is popular not only with divers, but also with fishing enthusiasts. Unfortunately, the result is a tangle of nets and ropes that envelopes the structure of the stern.*

E - The Romagna *was an oil tanker and had few structures on the deck. Most of them have been destroyed, except for this small cabin.*

F - The bow of the Romagna *is about 800 meters away from the hull. A large anchor, its fluke covered by sponges, pokes out of the right hawsehole.*

G - The entire wreck is surrounded by clouds of swallowtail sea perches (Anthias anthias) *small fish typical of deep shallows.*

H - The bow area is the most devastated. This is where the ship hit the mine, and where the explosion tore the tip of the ship completely off. The bow was further damaged by fires.

I - It is possible to visit some internal parts of the bow, a number of holds and the small cabin on the deck. Special safety measures are of course necessary to enter the ship, which should be explored only by very expert divers.

F

E

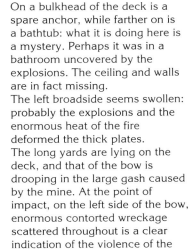

G

H

completely torn off.

On the sand before the bow sparse accumulations of materials are partially submerged and difficult to decipher. Here as well, an extraordinary concentration of black bristlestars cover the bottom: some are grouped on top of their prey. The stump of the bow is too far from the hull to reach during this dive, but if it were possible there would be no problems in orientation because a long strip of wreckage and fragments seems to connect the two pieces of the ship.

Another dive is necessary to see this part of the ship, and it is like diving on another wreck. It lies 43 meters deep and is enveloped by a cloud of red damselfish.

Here as well, the left side is torn apart, and the contorted wreckage shows the point of impact with the mine.

The right side looks like it was cut with a blowtorch, and from the hawsehole a long chain hangs to which the anchor is still attached, resting on the sandy seabed.

A couple of meters away a large moray pokes its head out from the wreckage. The small portion of deck remaining is covered with wood, like the hull of the *Romagna*. Inside the wreckage a good-sized school of large seabreams takes refuge.

Like all large sunken wrecks, the *Romagna* offers new discoveries and thrills with every dive.

On a bulkhead of the deck is a spare anchor, while farther on is a bathtub: what it is doing here is a mystery. Perhaps it was in a bathroom uncovered by the explosions. The ceiling and walls are in fact missing.

The left broadside seems swollen: probably the explosions and the enormous heat of the fire deformed the thick plates.

The long yards are lying on the deck, and that of the bow is drooping in the large gash caused by the mine. At the point of impact, on the left side of the bow, enormous contorted wreckage scattered throughout is a clear indication of the violence of the explosion. The right side seems

I

SCOGLIO DEL TORO

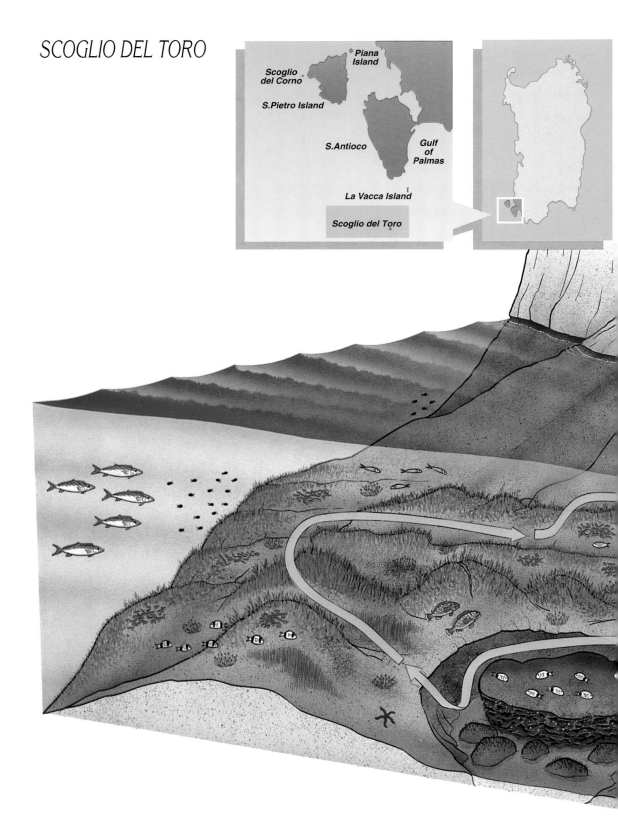

Piana Island

Scoglio del Corno

S.Pietro Island

S.Antioco

Gulf of Palmas

La Vacca Island

Scoglio del Toro

S.Antioco

Capo Sperone

La Vacca Island

N

Scoglio
del Toro

0m

10m

20m

26m

A little less than six miles south of S. Antioco lies the last bit of Sardinia: Scoglio del Toro. It is a large reef of volcanic rock, cone-shaped and almost completely bare. At its highest point there are a few timid signs of vegetation. On its northeast side the most exposed walls are yellow with lichen, and a stairway leads to a little white lighthouse on its summit. On the rocks at sea level live seagulls and a few cormorants, but the island is above all a stronghold of the eleonora falcon. A symbol of Mediterranean nature, this talkative dark falconet with its elegant flight actually comes to Sardinia, including Scoglio del Toro, Capo Sandalo di Carloforte and Capo di Monte Santu, only to nest in

A

Sphaerococcus, a highly branched red algae, known as gorgonian algae due to its bright red color, is quite common on the substratum. In the more sheltered areas a few sparse patches of Neptune grass grow with difficulty, often exhibiting leaves so short that they seem cut with a lawnmower: another sign of the extraordinary hydrodynamics of this area. Another particular condition caused by the currents is that many organisms which are normally relegated to dark areas, especially bryozoans, grow among the algae, often in direct light. Unusually large quantities of false coral and pentapora have colonized the horizontal rocks as well, adding another uncommon element. In

B

C

D

late summer, after which it returns to its winter residence near Madagascar. When sea conditions make it possible to reach the island, you cannot help but see and hear the hundreds of falcons that occupy the niches in the rocks and fly about in search of prey. The island rises up from a base that descends steeply, and which at a distance of two hundred meters from the rocks exceeds 50 meters in depth. You can dive anywhere, seeking shelter from the currents among the ridges that slope down into the water, continuing the profile of the emerged rocks. One of these ridges runs from the southeast point where the slope descends gradually. When you are underwater, you can not only directly feel the current, but

you discover that the current is the predominant force here, determining the composition of the organisms that cover the rocks. Brown algae in particular, but also green and red algae grow almost uniformly on the rocky ridges and are continuously agitated by the movement of the water. The surface layer is composed of a remarkable variety of species, all typical of powerful hydrodynamics: cystoseira, sargassum and *Dictyopteris* all have robust, branched thalli made especially to resist the force of currents. Cystoseira in particular is normally limited to the shallowest depths, yet here it grows down to a depth of 20 meters, a sure sign that the currents are quite powerful.

A - The more illuminated parts of the rocks are covered by a thick carpet of brown algae.

B - The seabeds of Scoglio del Toro are often swept by powerful currents, and can thus be visited only when the weather is good.

C - A large concentration of colonies of false coral (Miriapora truncata) grows on the summit of a rock.

D - Large encrusting sponges, probably Spirastrella cunctatrix, form colorful patches among the brown algae that cover the rocks.

E - The rocky seabed that slopes down to form walls and channels is covered by brown algae, beneath which is a carpet of encrusting red algae.

F - Many areas of the shallow are covered with brown algae from the genus Cistoseira, which grow luxuriantly here to a depth of more than 20 meters..

G - A close-up photo of a sargassum plant clearly shows its aerocysts, floating bladders full of gas that permit the plant to stand upright. Sargassum is typical of areas swept by currents.

H - A hermit crab (Dardanus arrosor) carries its load of sea anemones (Calliactis parasitica). This is a classic example of symbiosis.

I - An ornate wrasse (Thalassoma pavo) hunts for small invertebrates among the algae on the seabed. This small predator is quite common along the western coast of Sardinia.

certain areas the rock is bare due to grazing by sea urchins, and near the surface in less exposed areas some small orange corals can be seen. Descending along the slope, the rock alternates with ridges and gullies, where in the shadowy areas large orange sponges grow. Big spiny starfish, Marthasterias glacialis, are on the hunt, and the tentacles of large sea anemones poke out of the crevices. Everywhere little clouds of ornate wrasses contend with each other for food; while schools of saddled seabreams and salemas occupy different layers of the column of water. Around the peaks swarms of damselfish move jerkily. The little island is also an important transit point for large pelagic species. In

June, if you are lucky, you may see schools of amberjacks and bonitos passing by. The dive continues along the slope until you reach an area between 21 and 26 meters in depth, where the slope flattens out and little amphitheaters open up. The smallest masses on the seabed are encrusted with red algae, and under the largest rocks live large numbers of groupers, which normally can be seen nose down outside their lairs. You can go to the edge of the holes and watch these large serranidae turning elegantly. Ascend slowly as you come to other ridges and canals that cut into the crags of the slope, and as you reach the anchor you will find yourself once again surrounded by a swarm of damselfish.

F

G

H

I

BANCO POMATA

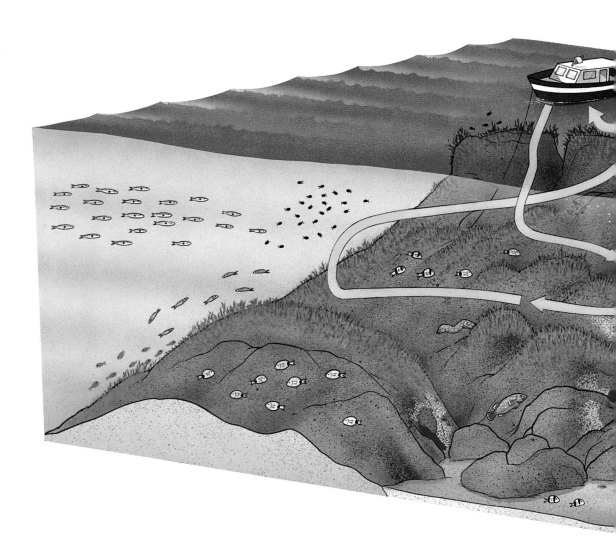

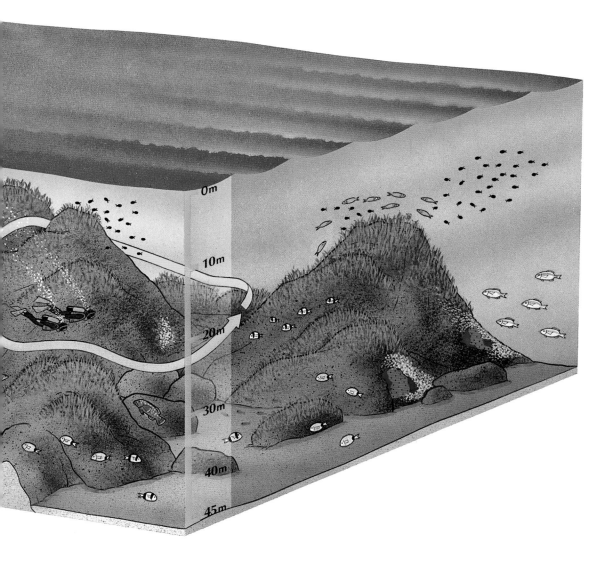

O ff the coast of Capo
Sperone on the island of
S. Antioco, facing westward, an area
of rocky reefs extends for some
distance out onto the seabed. As you
approach by boat, the impression of
being in the open sea is heightened
by the presence of shearwaters.
Groups of these marine birds patrol
the surface of the sea by skimming
the water in search of anchovies,
sardines and mackerel. You thus
reach the highest point of the reef,
lying 13 meters below the surface
and surrounded by various other
peaks at lower depths. A dive at
Banco Pomata begins on the highest
peak, which can easily be seen from
the surface when the sea is calm.
The shallow is almost always swept

A

algae cover the rocks, interrupted
here and there by areas grazed by
sea urchins. In particular you will
note brown algae such as *Padina*
and *Dictyopteris*, but if you look
carefully you may also spot the
fronds of a small sea-tangle bent by
the current. This is almost a rarity,
as these algae do not grow in many
areas of Sardinia and are in fact
extremely localized throughout the
Mediterranean basin. In less exposed
areas large orange patches of
sponges contend for space with
colonies of golden zoanthids. The
route takes you southeast toward
the mass, with the summit at 34
meters. The base of the mass of
rock is surrounded on all sides by a
rockslide that ends in the sand at a

B

C

D

by currents, which are sometimes
so powerful that the dive becomes
impossible. The lack of exact
references and the distance and
depth of the peaks also make it
inadvisable to dive in the current
with the boat following the divers.
So, if the day is good, dive down to
the highest rocks, which are always
surrounded by a dense cloud of
damselfish. As you descend along
the top you should always look
around you, as it is easy to spot
groups of amberjacks, seabreams,
and black seabreams. The jagged
slope of the shallow descends quite
deep, and you should check your
depth gauge often, as the clear water
may cause you to descend farther
than you should. Various species of

A - Secca di Banco Pomata is covered by a thick cloak of brown algae and is patrolled by swarms of ornate wrasses. Red stars (Ophidiaster ophidianus) are also common.

B - The most common aspect of dives at Banco Pomata is the almost constant presence of powerful currents.

C - Clouds of damselfish hover over the shallow, and sponges and golden zoanthids can be seen in the shadowy areas.

D - Lobsters are common in the crevices among the rocks. Shy during the day, by night they leave their hiding places in search of food, primarily dead animals.

E - A spiny starfish (Marthasterias glacialis) crawls among the tufts of brown and red algae and colonies of bryozoans.

F - A small red scorpionfish (Scorpaena notata) peeps out from the white fans of the peacock's tail alga (Padina pavonica).

G - The deeper portions of the shallow contain swarms of swallowtail sea perch (Anthias anthias): the individual pictured is a male.

H - Among the red algae, a dotted sea slug (Discodoris atromaculata) feeds on its favorite sponge (Petrosia ficiformis).

I - Many mullets swim among the algae and the patches of sand around the shallow.

depth of around 45 meters. From the summit you can see several groupers among the rocks on the seabed, where beautiful brown meagres also swim. Often groups of amberjacks on the hunt pass by. Around you are again damselfish and many anthias, in groups led by dominant males. Then return to the main slope, leaving a peak that rises up nearly 20 meters from the surface. In the crevices there are many large, common morays, conger eels, lobsters and porter crabs. As you ascend, there is time to observe even the smallest life forms, including various species of starfish such as the large *Ophidiaster,* molluscs (*Discodoris atromaculata*) grazing on their

E

favorite sponges, and numerous groups of ornate wrasses. Due to its distance from the coast and the structure of the shallow, this place gives one the peculiar sensation that anything could happen here, and for this reason it is altogether natural to find yourself looking around from time to time, scrutinizing the blue depths. However, you should also note the numerous fishing lines, ropes, cables and fish traps abandoned among the rocks by fishermen with scant respect for a fascinating environment so full of life. Even during your safety stop, life seems to swarm around you as ctenophores and other strange planktonic organisms float by gently, transported by the current.

F

G

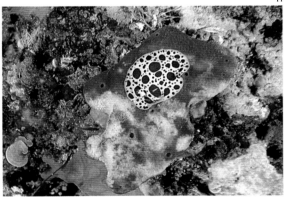

H

I

SCOGLIO
DEL CORNO

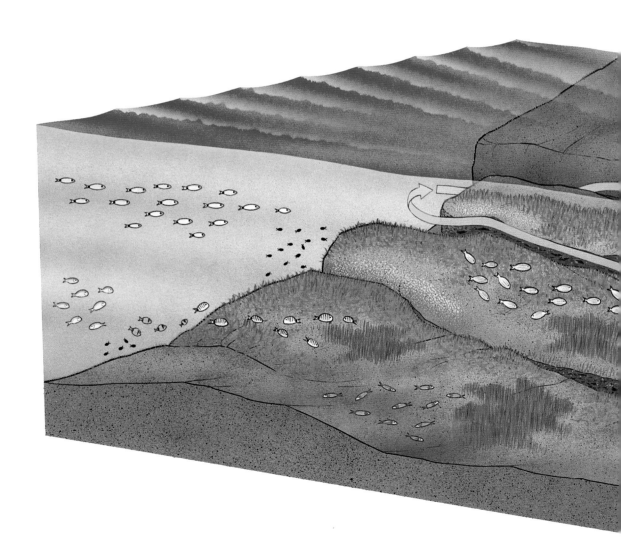

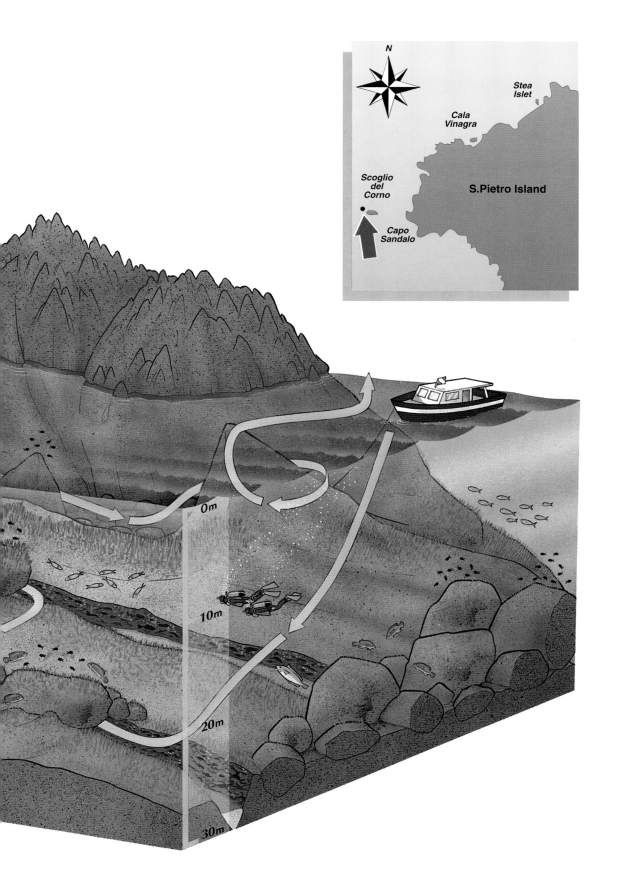

N

Stea
Islet

Cala
Vinagra

Scoglio
del
Corno

S.Pietro Island

Capo
Sandalo

0m

10m

20m

30m

To the west of Capo Sandalo, a little over a half mile out to sea, the Secca dell'Isolotto is a reef of dark volcanic rock, fretted and eroded by the waves. It rises from a seabed that descends rapidly, furrowed by deep gullies running east to west, like the emerged reef. The southern side descends more rapidly, turning into a large slope, while the northern side is less steep and descends in fits and starts, delimited by channels, the deepest of which is 40 meters deep, with walls embellished with small colonies of red coral. Moor wherever the wind is most favorable: if the scirocco is blowing, you should anchor near

the outermost point, where the current crosses and the islet creates a convenient shelter underwater.

Descend toward the third channel, which has a sandy floor about 30 meters deep. The rocks are covered by a large quantity of algae, especially brown algae but also large quantities of red algae as soon as the slope becomes more vertical.

From here the route is easy and quite varied, with constant surprises. The narrow sandy channel has short stretches of vertical walls, and rising toward the east, leads into several narrow passages among the large rocky masses, forming a roof.

Rays of light filter in from the fissures among the rocks that form the vault. Under the masses the walls are covered with large colorful patches of sponges, while big forkbeards and brown meagres swim from one hole to another. Leaving this first tunnel, ascend a bit until you come to the second channel, where you will immediately see another passage under an enormous rock.

It proceeds along the deep cleft carpeted with golden zoanthids, bryozoans and sponges on the eastern side. The channel ends almost at the end of the reef, and currents are quite likely. Patches of Neptune grass grow on the slopes, continuously breaking the algae cover. Immediately below the Neptune grass, as the light changes, the golden zoanthids reappear in dense colonies. From here turn right, following the rocks, and enter the first gully right below the emerging reef. To the left the wall is steep and rises to the surface.

The scene is rendered even more fascinating by the crashing of the waves. Swim through the narrow walls at a depth of about 15 meters: the floor of the channel is covered with masses and other fallen rocks, forming vaults and passages with beautiful plays of light. This is the reign of encrusting sponges in all colors, golden zoanthids, and, in the right season, squills. On the walls you will see various species of

A - Almost directly across from the lighthouse at Capo Sandalo on the island of S. Pietro is the dark form of Corno Islet, rising up a few meters from the water. In late summer numerous eleonora falcons can be seen flying over the rocks of the cape and the islet.

B - The submerged rocks around the islet descend in steps, and on the northwest side a pyramid-shaped spur rises almost to the surface, where the waves break.

C - To the west, the rocks of the islet are exposed to the open sea. Currents and waves are often quite strong, and are powerful forces in shaping the entire environment.

D - The channels which traverse the submerged rocks in steps are often covered by large masses of rock that form crevices and vaults. The more shadowy areas are covered with brightly colored sponges and luxuriant carpets of golden zoanthids.

nudibranchs, numerous dotted sea slugs and large *Platydoris argo*. If you keep a sharp eye you may spot perfectly camouflaged small spinous spider crabs, completely covered with algae, while morays peep out from the holes.

The last stretch of channel leads up to a rockslide and another passage behind a large pyramid-shaped rocky tooth, where you can make your safety stop as you watch the waves crashing above you. Around you swim various seabreams, including saddled seabreams and black seabreams, while ornate wrasses rummage through the algae. You may also see amberjacks and dentex patrolling the submerged ridges.

F

E

G

H

E - Several rocky masses rise up from the floor. They are covered by an almost unbroken carpet of large golden zoanthids.

F - The crumbled masses on the cracks that traverse the shallow form lovely passageways, where plays of light and shadow add to the colors of the corals and sponges.

G - Red algae, easily identifiable by their pinkish color, grow abundantly under the top layer of brown algae. Orange sponges provide an extra touch of color.

H - Among the great variety of algae that covers the submerged rocks are several species of Codium, *a green alga covered by a thick fuzz that gives it a velvety appearance.*

LE TACCHE BIANCHE

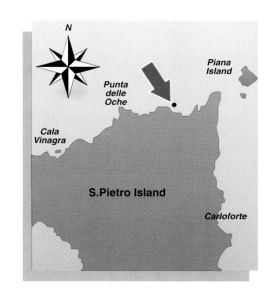

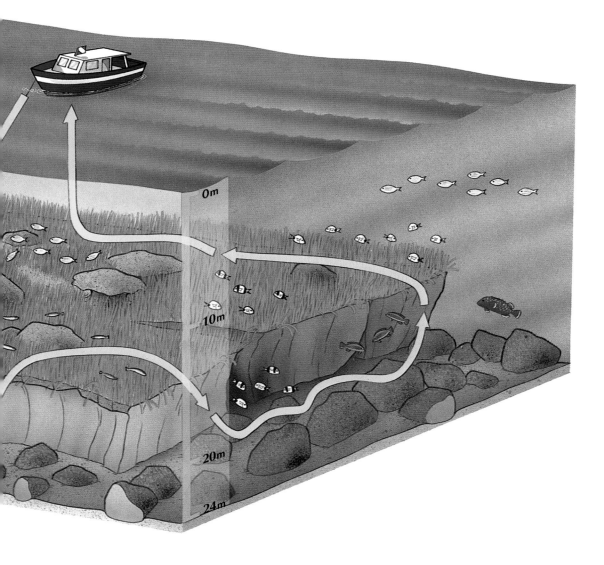

ailing along the coast of Carloforte from the east, after passing the tuna fisheries, still in partial use, you will note distant layers of light sedimentary rock standing out on the dark volcanic walls toward the northwest. This is Tacche Bianche, and it is the area where the tuna fishing nets were once located.

The present day tuna nets, which are once again in use, are set down in the spring only a few hundred meters farther east. Moor the boat about 200 meters from the shore, on a seabed which does not appear extremely attractive. At a depth of 18 meters a flat area covered by a dense meadow of Neptune grass is

interrupted here and there by scattered rounded masses and strange, mushroom-shaped rocky formations. Toward the open sea the plateau is broken by a rockslide of large square blocks of light rock which form an endless number of crevices. Descend along the mooring line and suddenly a large rounded opening with smooth walls appears in the meadow. Go in, and you will unexpectedly find yourself at the entrance to a large, wide tunnel that runs under the meadow. In various areas the vault has collapsed, and the masses that stand in the passage without blocking the wall permit light to enter. The floor of the tunnel

reaches a maximum depth of 24 meters and is covered by smooth rocks with pink patches of encrusting red algae that alternate with areas of light sand.

The walls and the vaults in the less illuminated areas are almost bare, while near the openings broad colorful patches of sponges appear. The tunnel is a favorite habitat of squills, which in late spring are quite common here. The tunnel continues for dozens of meters, with columns and other rockslides, until a pile of rocks closes the passageway and you come out onto the meadow above. As you come out, be careful of your movements, as it is easy to surprise not only the ever-present

A - Channels created by karst phenomena run under the surface covered by Neptune grass, while on the sea floor there are rocky masses and white sand. Large openings connect the two levels and create fascinating plays of light.

B - A number of light-colored sedimentary deposits stand out among the dark volcanic rocks on the north side of S. Pietro Island, known as Tacche Bianche.

C - The meadow of Neptune grass that covers the sea floor is broken by rockslides, and the colors explode at the base of the rocky masses. A red star crawls on a carpet of brightly-colored invertebrates.

D - The meadow of Neptune gras is inhabited by a myriad of fish and invertebrates.

E - These sea fans are small green algae typical of areas with poor illumination.

F - Every part of the meadow of Neptune grass is inhabited by organisms: a hermit crab crawls along its leaves, which have been colonized by red algae and bryozoans.

G - The sharpsnout seabream (Diplodus puntazzo) is easily distinguished from other seabreams by its clear vertical streaks and prominent mouth.

H - The blotched pickerel (Spicara maena) prefers Neptune grass meadows for its reproduction ground.

I - Cuttlefish are quite common in all shallow areas.

schools of salemas, but also a big gilt-head bream or a large common seabream.
The plateau hides other tunnels which are easily accessible, but be careful to check your computer often. The depth of the dive is constant and considering the maximum depth, downtime is rather brief and passes quite quickly as you wander through the tunnels. At the end of the plateau there is a sheer edge with smooth walls that connect numerous tunnels of various size. Here at the foot of the wall, among the rockslides and the crevices, beautiful groupers and large brown meagres can easily be seen. Seabreams also find shelter in the

deeper areas. While the lower level is quite interesting, so is the meadow above it, scattered with strange-shaped, eroded and fissured masses.
One of these looks like an airplane with wings and cockpit.
Green and rainbow wrasses, black seabreams and two-banded seabreams swim among the tufts of Neptune grass, and if you look for smaller species you will see crustaceans, tube dwelling anemones, sea anemones, spirographs, ascidians and bryozoans. Once again, an apparently monotonous, uninteresting environment reveals a rich variety in forms of life and unexpected seascapes.

F

G

H

I

S'ARCHITTU

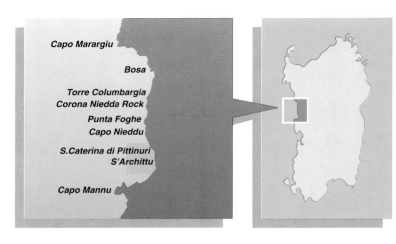

Capo Marargiu

Bosa

Torre Columbargia
Corona Niedda Rock
Punta Foghe
Capo Nieddu

S.Caterina di Pittinuri
S'Archittu

Capo Mannu

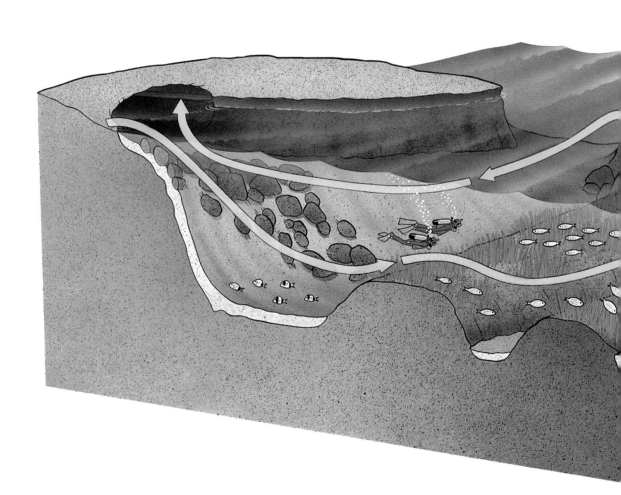

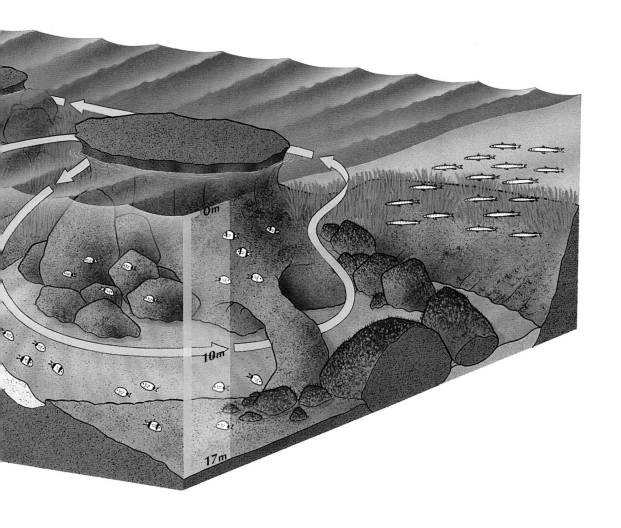

S.Caterina di Pittinuri

Torre del Pozzo

Is Arenas

N

0m

10m

17m

A

A - The promontory of S'Archittu juts out to the north of the Sinis Peninsula. The sandstone that forms it has been eroded by the waves and the sea. The dive begins right under the natural arch.

B - The erosion phenomena that have transformed the rocks in the area are evident under water as well. Vaults, tunnels and channels can be seen that make the dive quite varied and beautiful.

C - Neptune grass colonizes many channels among the rocks, and sometimes grows luxuriantly even above the blocks of sandstone. The abrupt transition from the Neptune grass to the red algae is quite striking.

D - A horse pipefish (Sygnatus typhle) shows off its extraordinary mimetic skills, not only standing erect, like the leaves of the Neptune grass, but also faithfully reproducing its color.

E - A sea lily distends its arms among a pile of dead Neptune grass leaves, in another quite remarkable feat of mimicry.

B

C

Walls of sandstone begin as you head north up the coast past Sinis, passing the large sandy inlet of Is Arenas.
The rock has been sculpted by the wind and water, and the symbol of the coastal landscape of this area is S'Archittu, a large natural vault traversed from end to end by the sea. The dive begins right here, from the land side of the tunnel. Descend a few meters deep, passing rapidly from a well-illuminated environment to the tunnel, where red algae thickly coats the walls and the floor. Sand and smooth rock masses show signs of strong hydrodynamics, and the sediment is distributed in parallel waves.
The red algae are primarily coralline, with various encrusting species. The long tunnel is lovely, especially due to the light that enters from the two entrances. It leads out onto a sandy flat area surrounded by thick patches of Neptune grass. The long diving route begins here, through channels, vaults and passage holes, leading around the two emerging reefs just off from the cape.
The seabed, like the rest of the surrounding area, is marked by the erosion processes which affected the coast when it lay above water. Remains of karst conduits form beautiful passages carved in the crumbling rocks, where erosion continues with the constant currents. The higher zones are covered with Neptune grass, which has also colonized many sandy channels. Heart urchins, especially those from the genus *Echinocardium*, live buried in the sediment, with their thin exoskeleton covered with thick hairs. Go past the first rise, where thick schools of salemas graze on the Neptune grass. Then head left to a channel 12 meters deep, and come to the side of the largest emerging reef facing the shore. To the side of the reef a hole leads into a vertical well with a floor about 14 meters deep, covered by large smooth stones. Exit from a vault covered with golden zoanthids. Move with caution, as it is not uncommon to encounter amberjacks, leer-fish or even bass.

D

Right as you exit go around a pile of masses at the base of the reef, to enter into another channel with a sandy floor. The walls are covered with corals, and on the edges grow numerous colonies of hydrozoans. Just a little farther up is the Neptune grass meadow that borders the sciophilous areas. The channel is interrupted by an arch: after crossing it you will see scattered masses, where white seabreams and two-banded seabreams are swimming. Turn left again and, after crossing

F - A colorful sea slug (Tylodina perversa) feeds on its favorite sponge (Aplysina aerophoba). The slug is unmistakable due to its showy yellow color and its pagoda-shaped shell.

E

H

F

another nearby arch, on the wall of the reef you will see a rise covered with Neptune grass. Go past it and, going around the rock, head back, aiming for the other small emerging reef.

Come out toward the shore and go to the wall that once again leads under the tunnel you started from, go back along it and come out on the shallows.

The most entertaining aspect of this dive is the continuing variety of the seascape and the many passages among the rocks. Moreover, it is an extremely easy dive, although you should always be careful of your position in the channels and tunnels.

There is much to see. For those interested in nudibranchs, some uncommon species such as *Berghia caerulescens* and *Calmella cavolinii*, two small, colorful members of the Eolidacea family, are common here. On the walls of the channels you may also see some beautiful lobsters.

But the crowning touch, if you are lucky, could be a fine school of barracudas.

G - The pearly razor fish (Xyrichthys novacula) lives in patches of sand. Its fine colors appear evanescent against the sand. The pearly razor fish often hides in the sand to escape from predators.

H - Sea anemones (Anemonia sulcata) are common in the meadows and among the rocks. Sea anemones can become quite large: the crown of tentacles is always visible, while the column is hidden.

SU PUNTILLONE

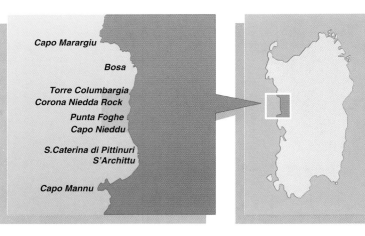

Capo Marargiu

Bosa

Torre Columbargia
Corona Niedda Rock
Punta Foghe
Capo Nieddu

S.Caterina di Pittinuri
S'Archittu

Capo Mannu

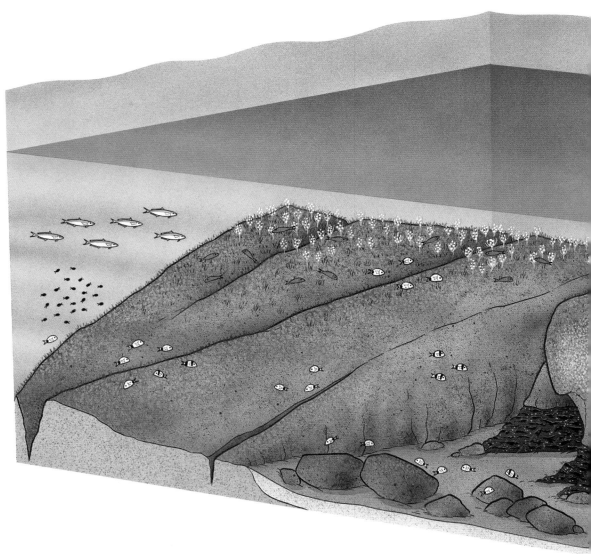

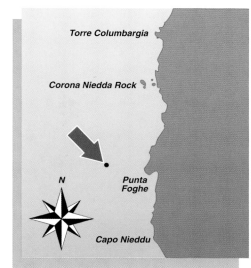

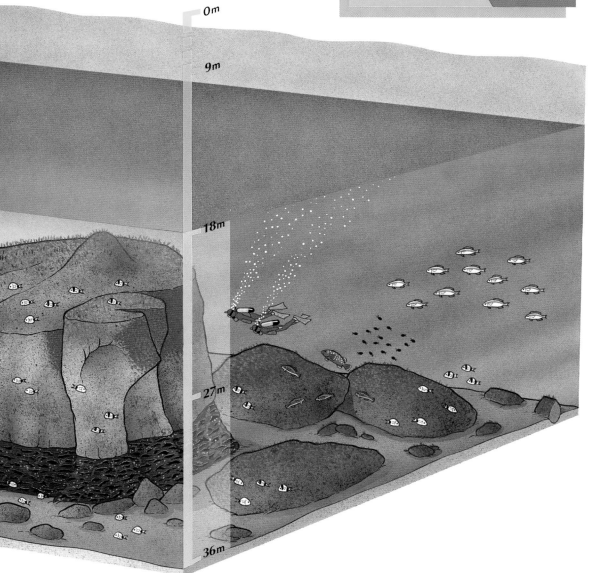

North
of Punta Foghe,
about two and a half
miles out to sea at a depth of forty
meters bathymetric line is an area
of rocks where the summit of the
largest reef rises to a depth of 19
meters. It is called Su Puntillone,
probably because of the sharp
peak that signals it on sonic depth
finders. Moor at the highest area,
where the clear water often makes
it possible to see the rocks even
from the surface.
The north and west sides of the

C

A

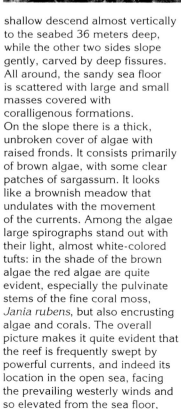

D

shallow descend almost vertically
to the seabed 36 meters deep,
while the other two sides slope
gently, carved by deep fissures.
All around, the sandy sea floor
is scattered with large and small
masses covered with
coralligenous formations.
On the slope there is a thick,
unbroken cover of algae with
raised fronds. It consists primarily
of brown algae, with some clear
patches of sargassum. It looks
like a brownish meadow that
undulates with the movement
of the currents. Among the algae
large spirographs stand out with
their light, almost white-colored
tufts: in the shade of the brown
algae the red algae are quite
evident, especially the pulvinate
stems of the fine coral moss,
Jania rubens, but also encrusting
algae and corals. The overall
picture makes it quite evident that
the reef is frequently swept by
powerful currents, and indeed its
location in the open sea, facing
the prevailing westerly winds and
so elevated from the sea floor,
seems to dictate such a situation.

B

C - The flat area
of the shallow is
covered by a layer
of algae with
raised fronds: this
is known as
sargassum
(Sargassum
vulgare).
Numerous round
bladders grow
among its thalli,
which are similar
to leaves,
permitting the
plant to stand
erect.

D - Numerous
spirographs
(Sabella
spallanzani) with
nearly white tufts
stand out in the
meadow of
sargassum,
surrounded by
rainbow wrasses
and damselfish.

E - The walls
covered with jewel
anemones are
exposed to the
prevailing currents.
These animals are
in fact typical of
areas with strong
hydrodynamics.

These conditions are also favorable for the passage of large pelagic species, including amberjacks and dentex, which offer spectacular sights if you are fortunate enough to dive on the right day.

The sheer side of the shallow is quite different. Right at the edge a cloak of red algae begins in which sea roses predominate.

There are also numerous indicators of powerful hydrodynamics: sea anemones of all sizes, from tiny glass bell tunicates to large rock violets, carpet the walls, alternating with violet *Haliclona mediterranea* sponges. But what most characterizes the shallow and what makes it quite special is the presence of a myriad of jewel anemones (*Corynactis viridis*), which despite their scientific name are a beautiful bright lilac color. For Sardinia at least, this is a rare and extraordinarily beautiful spectacle: the small anemones are mixed with sponges, sea anemones and red algae and

F

F - Jewel anemones are cnidarians which belong to a special order, the Corallimorpharia. The crown of tentacles is less than one centimeter in diameter, and each tentacle ends in a round swelling.

G

G - The walls of the shallow offer shelter to a great variety of organisms, like these corals, which have a body protected by a calcareous skeleton.

H - The micro-environments of the shallow include an intricate group of organisms from various groups, all contending for living space: sponges, jewel anemones, bryozoans and algae create a complicated palette of colors.

E

H

peculiarity of this dive: the elongated fronds of a sea tangle. This is an algae from the genus *Phyllariopsis* which generally lives at a depth of around 40 meters. Continuing along the side of the shallow, the wall becomes sheer, and here is the point where the jewel anemones are most numerous, and where the scenery is the most beautiful, with the high part of the shallow surrounded by a dense cloud of damselfish.

The wall ends in a deep cleft that separates from the slope where the dive began. Returning toward the anchor, among the algae you can see glass bell tunicates and various species of nudibranchs, especially *Flabellina ischitana*, *Coryphella pedata* and *Discodoris atromaculata*. From here emerge back near the boat, continuing to look around: curious amberjacks may approach, but there may also be a chance to see beautiful comb jellies and many other planktonic creatures passing quickly by as they are carried by the current.

provide an uncommonly exotic touch to the dive. Moreover, right in the middle of the lilac colored anemones, a tiny area of wall is covered by an extremely strange, lemon-yellow colored variety with black tentacles. At least it appears that way: your flashlight beam will transform the yellow into lime green, or viridis, and the black

into bright red.
Swimming at a depth of 27 meters, pass the vertical wall, keeping it on your left.
On the sea floor around the large masses you can see brown meagres, forkbeards and schools of two-banded seabreams.
If you come down onto the masses you can see another

CORONA NIEDDA

Capo Marargiu

Bosa

Torre Columbargia
Corona Niedda Rock

Punta Foghe
Capo Nieddu

S.Caterina di Pittinuri
S'Archittu

Capo Mannu

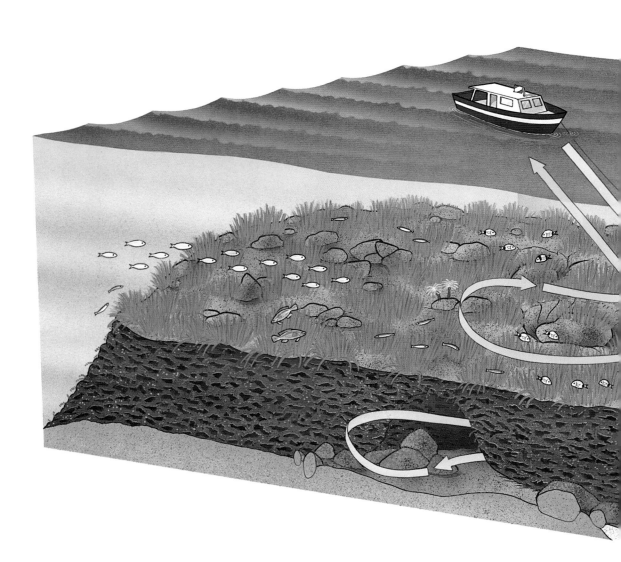

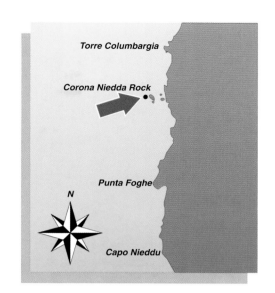

Torre Columbargia

Corona Niedda Rock

Punta Foghe

N

Capo Nieddu

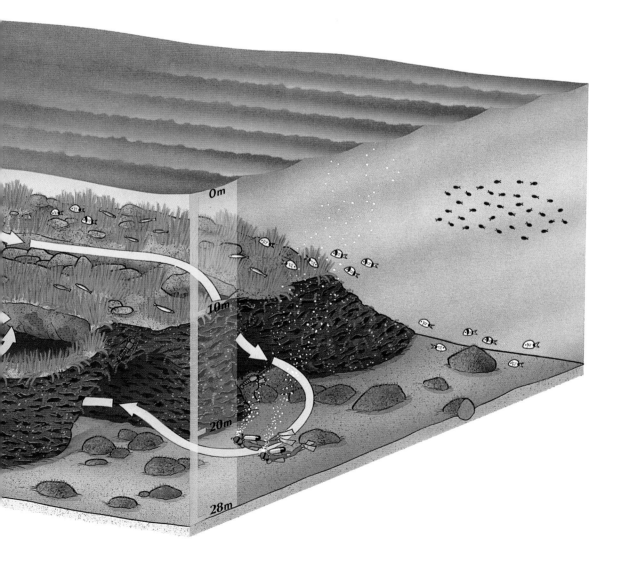

0m

10m

20m

28m

A

B

C

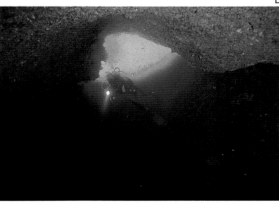

D

For some distance the coast between Punta Foghe and Bosa is a vertical bastion of volcanic rock, from which a group of high, jagged reefs and two lower ones extend. The whole area is known as Isolotto of Corona Niedda, and it is inhabited only by a large colony of green cormorants. Moor at the reef, three hundred meters off from the largest rocks. This is a rocky emerging area with an elongated form facing west, with its northern and southern sides sloping gently, while the outer side ends with almost vertical walls. The plateau on which you descend is 14 meters deep and consists of a group of scattered rocks interrupted by small patches of Neptune grass.

E

Head out to sea, and at the end of the shallow a small well leads under a rock arch that comes out ten meters farther down at the seabed, approximately 27 meters deep. The edge of the rise is covered with beautiful coral formations that create crevices and small terraces on which tufts of Neptune grass grow. In this complex environment it is common to see beautiful lobsters, with squat lobsters and common lobsters hiding in the crevices. The wall often descends vertically, and there are many things to see: sponges from the genus *Axinella* are quite common, very often colonized by golden zoanthids, just as the textbooks show. The concretions of algae are

F

dark, has bare rocks, the walls of the well should be observed centimeter by centimeter due to the great variety of organisms that have colonized it. Small but numerous colonies of coral hang from the small vaults formed by the coralligenous algae. Corals appear at 22 meters deep among sponges, sea anemones and bryozoans: many colonies have their polyps expanded in order to collect the sediment that falls from above. Going back up, there are increasing numbers of sea roses, and the illumination gradually increases up to the edge of the well, which is colonized by Neptune grass that covers the entire side of the shallow.

The Neptune grass is growing on a coralligenous base full of crevices: colorful nudibranchs, especially *Coryphella pedata* and *Flabellina ischitana*, graze on the hydrozoans which grow thickly on the algae of the seabed. This species has only recently been classified, and was in fact first described in the early 1990's. In all probability it was previously confused with its relative *Flabellina affinis* or with *Coryphella pedata*, which is quite similar in color and form, but is distinguished by having two smooth rhinophores with no annuli. The dive ends as you swim to the highest part of the shallow, where rainbow wrasses and peacock wrasses wander in search of food.

G

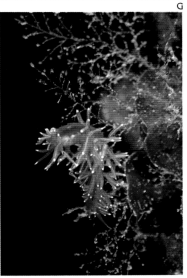

H

I

covered by an almost uniform layer of sea roses, and *Sphaerococcus coronopifolius* is quite common. Following the edge of the reef, on some stretches of the sea floor there are accumulations of a red algae (*Vidalia volubilis*) with a peculiar form, with a ribbon-like spiral-shaped thallus. Farther on, you will see a vault that leads into a cave with two exits. On the left a tunnel invites you to explore the deep side of the shallow, while the other is a vertical well about ten meters high and at least 4-5 meters in diameter. This the most spectacular part of the dive: the light that enters from the three openings creates beautiful patterns. But while the horizontal tunnel, which is almost completely

J

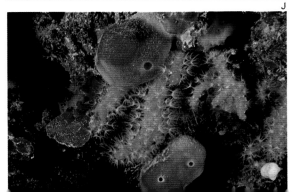

G - The conduits and the shaft are traversed by currents which favor the growth of hydrozoans. Colonies of these cnidarians, which live on red algae from the genus Peyssonellia, *are preyed upon by nudibranch gastropod mollusks (*Flabellina ischitana*).*

*H - Various species of red algae grow under the Neptune grass. In areas where hydrodynamics are present, gorgonian algae (*Sphaeroccus coronopifolius*), which owe their name to the red branches of the thallus, can be found.*

*I - The stony sea urchin (*Paracentrotus lividus*) is quite common among the fronds of Neptune grass. It grazes on algae with soft thalli, which it pulls off using a complex mouth apparatus.*

J - The walls of the vertical shaft favor the growth of red coral. Its expanded polyps are white and contrast with its red skeleton.

111

THE NORTHERN COAST: FROM ALGHERO TO MORTORIO

The stretch of coast from Bosa to Alghero is one of the wildest areas of the entire island. The most interesting point is Capo Maragiu, with its outlying shallows. Here, on the walls dropping sheer to the sea, lives the largest colony of griffin vultures in Sardinia. It is a spectacle of wild beauty to see the griffins, often in large groups, wheeling over the cliffs and sea with their enormous wings outspread in a span nearly three meters wide, riding up on the currents of warm air as they patrol the coast in search of food.
An extremely interesting diving area is located beyond Alghero. Between Punta Giglio and the coast of Capo Caccia, the earth plunges into the sea, and high walls surround the deep bay of Porto Conte. The limestone promontories and coast contain imposing karst phenomena which have perforated and carved out the rock both on land and underwater. Here the signs of the evolution of the coastline are evident and important: they provide spectacular and unequivocal documentation of the relationship between land and sea. First of all, there is the Grotta Verde (Green Grotto), closed to visitors, which opens out many meters above sea level on the eastern side of Capo Caccia.

A - The lighthouse overlooks the vertical cliff of Capo Caccia: the promontory at its base is Punta dell'Asino. In the background to the left, the island of Foradada rises up vertically a short distance from the coast. A marine reserve is planned for the Capo Caccia area.

B - Punta Sardegna, in the Palau area, plunges into the sea toward the Strait of Bonifacio and the La Maddalena Archipelago. The whole island is part of a recently established national park.

C - The coast of Spargi is characterized by low scrub alternating with wind-sculpted granite.

Its cavities contain one of the most important testimonies to prehistoric civilization on Sardinia. In the 1970's some of the most extraordinary underwater archeological research in the world took place here. About 7,000 years ago, when the sea level was a few meters below the present level, the grotto, now partially submerged, was used by the ancient inhabitants of the Capo as a burial place for their dead and their funeral trappings. There is one other discovery, just as important and surprising. In one of the many submerged caves a large group of bones of various species of mammals from the Quaternary period was found: the perfectly preserved remains of stags, canines, and small rodents are incorporated in the limestone just a little below the present-day sea level, a further testimony to the changes which have caused the evolution of the coast. The area of Punta Giglio and Capo Caccia is a paradise of underwater caves, with at least ten accessible to divers. Be careful, however, because dives in caves require special safety measures which cannot be neglected. Punta Giglio and Capo Caccia also mean coral: the legendary red gold grows in every crevice here just as soon as the light dims under the cliffs. It is not necessary to dive to any great depth to see red colonies of this precious colonizing animal. Even at 5-6 meters deep, the rock is literally covered with coral branches, not large, of course,

but nevertheless thrilling. Coming up and going north, passing the islands of Foradada and Piana, the coast continues high and sheer to the sea until Ghisciera. Right before Punta Cristallo it rises to 326 meters with a spectacular vertical cliff. Passing Argentiera, from Porto Palmas to Capo Falcone there is no trace of human settlement. Even the appearance of the rock changes and becomes darker, consisting primarily of schist. This entire stretch of the coast is exposed to prevailing third and fourth quadrant winds: sea storms are frequent, and the conformation of the coastal rocks and the remains of many sunken ships testify to the violence of the forces in play. Capo Falcone is across from the island of Asinara, now highly restricted due to the prison located there. In the near future, however, the island seems destined to become a natural park. When this occurs the seabeds which surround it, now accessible to only a few fortunate divers with the right

D

E

D - The Capo Testa promontory is surrounded by emerging rocks and shallows which can be seen from above. When the mistral is blowing, the rocks of the cape are swept by waves.

E - The whole Gallura coastal area is surrounded by small islands and rocks. These are extremely important and fragile ecosystems

F - The twisted, punctured and smoothed granite formations on the island of Mortorio contrast with the low green scrub of flowering rock rose. Mortorio Island and the others that surround it are part of La Maddalena National Park.

C

F

connections, will certainly become a great attraction for divers. From Capo Falcone to Castelsardo, the coast is low and sandy. Extremely long beaches face the great Gulf of Asinara. To find rocks you need to go back up to Rossa Island and then to Costa Paradiso. From there to Capo Testa the coral reappears, and in Bocche di Bonifacio it is still fished by the few remaining coral

boats. Capo Testa is surrounded by a group of shallows, perfectly visible as you survey the cape, but often inaccessible due to the sea and current. Indeed, Bocche di Bonifacio is a strait where winds and currents accelerate, often creating gale conditions, and the forms of the rocks of the cape and the coast, carved away by the wind and the waves, are eloquent

testimony to their violence. A little to the east beyond Capo Falcone is the wreck of the Marmorata. Another sunken ship, the Greek freighter *Angelika*, was until a short time ago easily identifiable by its masts emerging from the sea. Now they have collapsed, and the whole wreck is rapidly deteriorating. The entire La Maddalena archipelago is full of wrecks: submarines, torpedo boats, cargo ships and airplane motors. Unfortunately, they are almost all in deep water, often well below depths of 40 meters. Among the many islands of the archipelago there are dozens of very beautiful shallows full of gorgonians and granite seascapes with majestic vaults, as well as beautiful dives off the coast on the side sheltered from the mistral at Caprera. Towards the west the extensive Secca dei Monaci is the westernmost part of this area and one of the most interesting parts of the entire island. Descending south and passing Costa Smeralda, there is the little archipelago of Mortorio, where the most interesting dives are on the eastern side looking out to sea.

NEREO CAVE

The drawing of Nereo Cave is based on the original relief by V. Piras, R. Congiu, A. Addis.

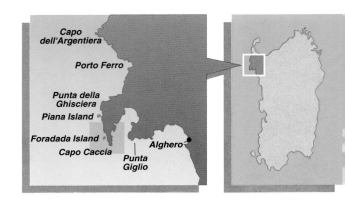

Capo dell'Argentiera

Porto Ferro

Punta della Ghisciera

Piana Island

Foradada Island

Capo Caccia

Punta Giglio

Alghero

LONGITUDINAL SECTION

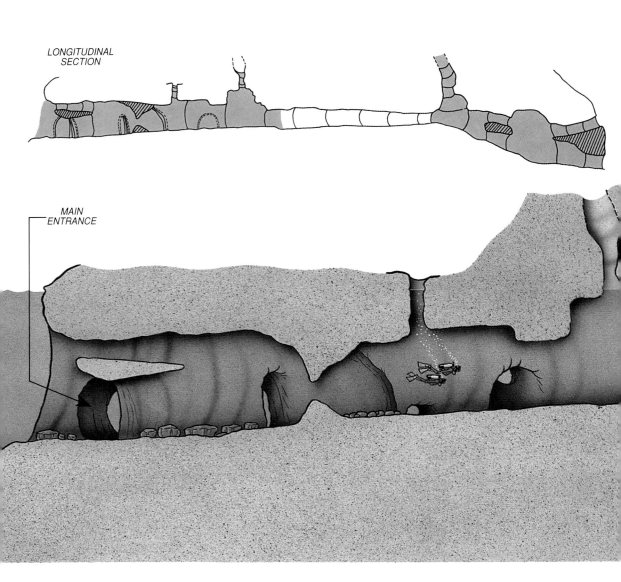

MAIN ENTRANCE

Piana Island

Porto Conte

Foradada Island

Punta Giglio

Capo Caccia

N

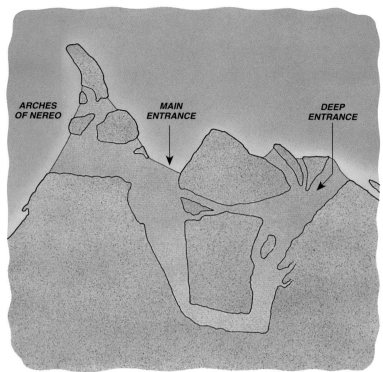

ARCHES OF NEREO

MAIN ENTRANCE

DEEP ENTRANCE

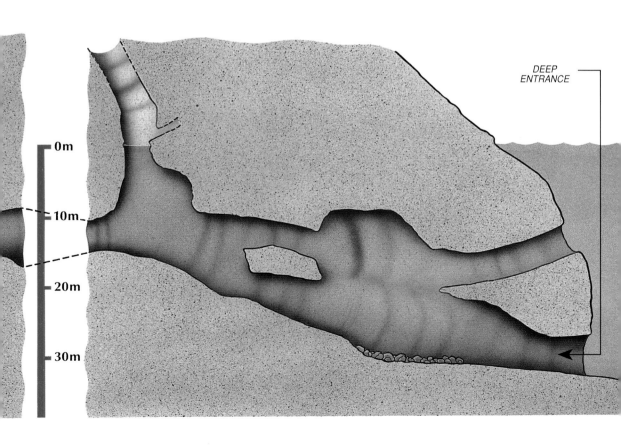

DEEP ENTRANCE

0m

10m

20m

30m

A

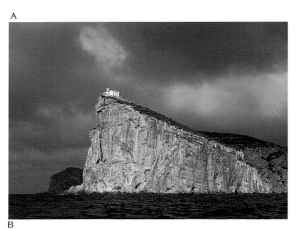

B

C

A short distance from Capo Caccia, where the vertical cliff turns north, is Punta dell'Asino, a rocky promontory that juts out from the wall. Below, on both sides of the spur, is the main entrance to Nereo Cave with its highly complex structure. The cave is probably the largest underwater cavity in Europe and perhaps in the world. It is over 350 meters long and in some points the vault is almost ten meters high. The group of tunnels has another outlet near Scoglio del Sommergibile (Submarine Rock) farther north. The route within the promontory is not straight and has various horizontal branches and two narrow chimneys above sea level, probably with subaerial communications. There are three main entrances. The first faces the cape and is the most classic and majestic, with a floor 20 meters deep. The second is perhaps more spectacular: the great openings form arches penetrated by rays of light that illuminate the large masses resting on the seabed 18 meters deep. The third is 32 meters deep and leads to a large cavern

A - The promontory of Capo Caccia is a limestone mass that plunges into the sea from north to south. The rocks are perforated by a myriad of cavities both above and below sea level. Underwater, the most classical dive is at Nereo Cave.

B - Nereo Cave has three major entrances: the largest is the opening that crosses Punta dell'Asino. This diver seems to be vanishing into the great blue hole of the cavern.

C - Next to the main entrance are small conduits from which sunlight gleams. Light conditions vary with the season, but the best time to dive is in the early afternoon.

D

from which various branches lead to the other two entrances. This side of the cave, facing almost north, is less illuminated than the other side. Except for these areas, the rest of the cave with its inner tunnels is completely dark, and special stratagems and proper organization are required in order to visit it. The large cavities that penetrate Punta dell'Asino make it possible to make a memorable dive, both in terms of scenery and the quantity of organisms typical of dark areas. Once the vaults that lead into the

D - Red coral covers the outer portions of the caverns of Capo Caccia, forming lovely carpets. The colonies and their expanded polyps seem surrounded by mist. The corals of Nereo Cave have remained intact in only a few areas.

cave were completely covered with red coral, but uncontrolled fishing has left only a few colonies in a few points of the cavern, and among the sediments on the floor only a few fragments remain of what must have been a true treasure, hundreds of kilos of fossil coral fallen from the vault. Descending along the cliff to the largest opening and entering the cavern, you will see a continuous sequence of changes in the composition of the organisms that cover the rock as illumination gradually decreases. On the outside on the masses on the sea floor, covered with a low mantle of photophilic algae, salemas graze and saddled seabreams and other breams swim about. On the walls where the tunnels open out there is a typical cliff environment with moderately sciophilous algae such as sea cactus and sea fans. The succession continues, with golden zoanthids which are then replaced by *Leptosammia pruvoti*: among these, in addition to the sparse branches of coral, are jumbles of sponges, bryozoans, annelids and sea anemones, while the algae

disappears completely in the absence of light. At the entrance of the conduits there are large rock violets (*Microcosmus sp.*) with an almost unrecognizable rough body, covered as they are with other animals, especially sponges. Specialized predators like the little *Hypselodoris tricolor* graze on the sponges, while the nudibranch gastropod *Discodoris atromaculata* grazes on *Petrosia*, which in the cave environment appears whitish due to the absence of the symbiotic algae present when there is light. This is also the typical environment for many crustaceans such as the porter crab with its robust pink claws, which grow quite large here, spiny lobsters, *Herbstia condyliata* crabs, and squat lobsters. In the inner areas live large lobsters and narval shrimp, elegant with their long beaks and fine white antennae and sometimes gathering in large crowds. In the cave there are also cleaning stations for the banded shrimp (*Stenopus spinosus*) with its long white antennae. Seen only in dark caves, this shrimp offers its services to complacent, quite large

H - Leptosammia pruvoti *is a coral typical of poorly illuminated areas and covers entire walls at the entrance to cavities* and crevices. Each individual has a hard calcareous skeleton, with the same yellow color as its tentacles.

G

H

E - A small red scorpionfish (Scorpaena notata) *camouflages itself against the rock. Like larger scorpionfish, it uses mimicry both as a defense and to make itself invisible to prey.*

F - A porter crab (Dromia personata) *moves along the wall of a cavern in Nereo Cave. Its name comes from the fact that, especially when small, it carries a fragment of sponge on its carapace which it uses to hide itself.*

G - Dark cavities are a typical habitat of cardinal fish (Apogon imberbis), *swarms of which occupy them.*

E

F

brown meagres that occupy several deep recesses in the cave. Another exclusive inhabitant of caves is a small brown fish with a snub nose: it is known as *Oligopus ater*, and as may be guessed, its name describes it well. *Oligopus* comes from the fact that instead of having distinct dorsal, caudal and anal fins like other fish, it has a single large fin that goes from back to stomach. *Ater* comes from its nearly black color. In addition to these animals capable of movement, all the sedentary organisms which live on the walls are either suspension feeders or filtrators: that is, they use different systems to collect the particles carried in by the current, and release waste that falls onto the seabed. This explains the presence of large tube-dwelling anemones, encouraged by the continuous fall of fine material. The cave holds surprises by night as well. Often large dentex come in from the open sea to sleep in the cavities, and this is the only time when these mysterious pelagic predators will permit divers to approach.

SECCA DI PORTO LECCIO

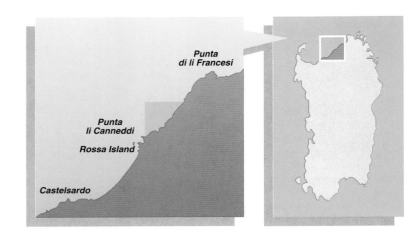

Punta di li Francesi

Punta li Canneddi

Rossa Island

Castelsardo

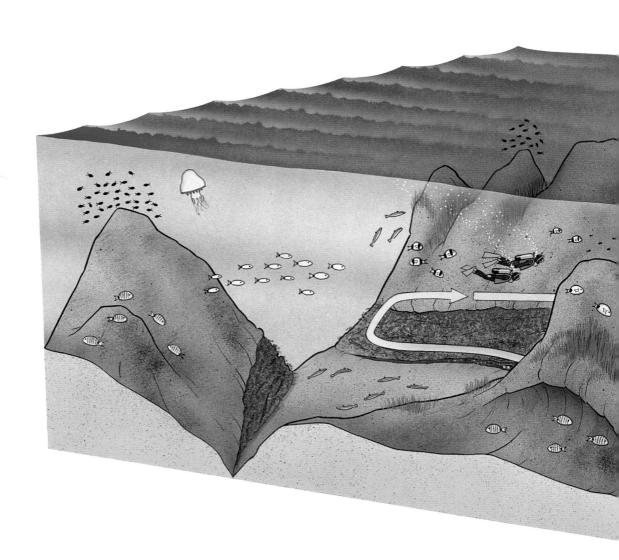

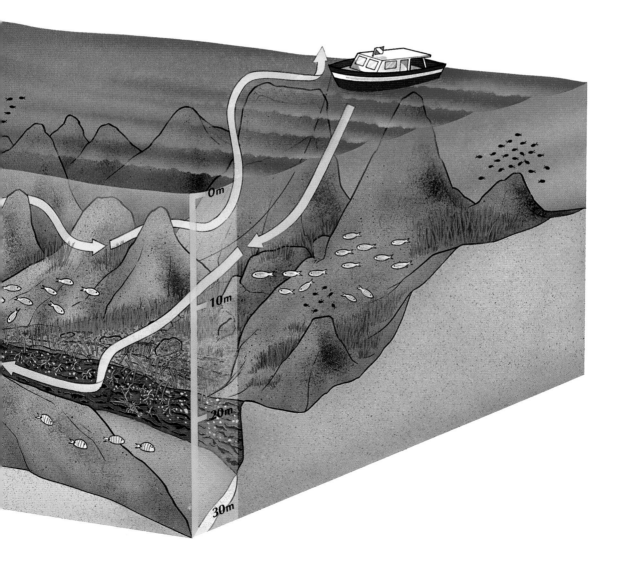

A

B

C

D

osta Paradiso is a tourist resort located on the northern coast between Castelsardo and Vignola. The coast is rocky and jagged, with reddish granite interrupted by low vegetation that surrounds small sandy inlets. A rocky promontory, surrounded by rocks and emerging shallows, protrudes out to sea between the bay of Li Cossi and that of Porto Leccio. To the west of the point several submerged peaks rise to 3 meters from the surface: this is where you should throw your anchor. The two tallest spurs are close to each other and divided by a trough that makes them look like two horns. This is why the place is also known as Secca del Vichingo.

E

Between the two peaks you will first encounter rocky masses, then, turning to the right, the sea floor widens and, at a depth from ten to twenty meters, there is a strange mixture of patches of Neptune grass and a coralligenous seabed with deep cracks, fissures and holes. The superficial layer is formed by sea cactus, and right below it is an imposing mass constructed by red algae. The short descent leads to a deeper area on the sand, to a depth of 31 meters. To the left, however, from twenty meters down and deeper, the wall descends vertically and leads into a narrow channel with a sandy bottom. The other side of the channel is formed by the base of

A - Most of the dive at Secca di Porto Leccio is along a deep channel with walls covered by large coralligenous formations.

B - The upper portion of the shallow is colonized by sparse patches of Neptune grass.

C - The uppermost rocks of the shallow are frequented by large schools of salemas, which graze among the algae.

D - The less exposed areas of the channel are covered by a layer of red algae, especially sea roses. Throughout the dive, the transition from illuminated to shaded areas is marked by abrupt changes i n environment.

E - The decrease in light from the upper portion of the shallow to the central channel is evident, making a flashlight necessary.

F - Beautiful colonies of red coral grow among the red algae on the walls.

G - The coralligenous environment includes an intricate combination of organisms heaped on top of each other. The green thalli of the sea cactus grow above them all.

H - A female black-faced blenny (Trypterigion tripteronotus) hovers motionless among the algae in wait of small prey.

I - The lobster's preferred habitat is within the coralligenous crevices .

another rocky emergence which is overlooked by a pointed spur that rises to a depth of 7 meters. The walls of the channel are carpeted with concretions of red algae. In fact, the light fades almost abruptly, creating a very particular situation. The edge of the channel is in part colonized by Neptune grass, and right under the roots of the phanerogams grows red coral. The small colonies of coral are quite numerous in the crevices and under the vaults, along with a large variety of other organisms typical of dark areas: sponges, bryozoans and annelids carpet every bit of available space, even climbing on top of each other. This is also a common habitat for spiny lobsters:

dozens of antennae poke out of the holes, and some of them belong to quite large specimens. Among the sponges you can see various species of nudibranchs, squat lobsters barely poke out from the fissures, while in the deeper holes, especially in early summer, you can see squills. Keep an eye on your gauge and computer as you cross the channel, because you are exploring at a depth of 27 meters, and there are so many things to see that it is easy to lose track of time. Ascend along a cleft covered with corals, crossed by a fissure where you can see seabreams and conger eels. As you reach shallower depths, at the base of the peaks between 10 and 15 meters deep, large schools of

salemas, seabreams and beautiful saddled seabreams swim among patches of Neptune grass and coral and emerged rocks. On the various species of algae you are likely to encounter small grazing species: sea slugs from the Sacoglossa order, like the brightly colored *Thuridilla hopei* and the mimetic *Elysia viridis*. The latter favors the branching fronds of codium algae, a dark green algae covered with thick fuzz. Before leaving the water, your safety stop is a stroll from the top of one peak to another. This is a good way to enjoy the quite lively scene, to spot groups of jellyfish rocking gently, and, if you have a sharp eye, to see tiny nudibranchs hidden in the niches in dimmer areas.

THE WRECK
OF THE ANGELIKA

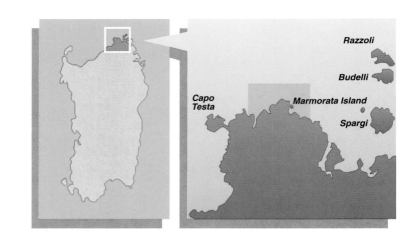

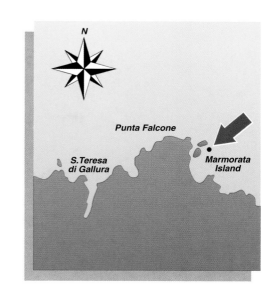

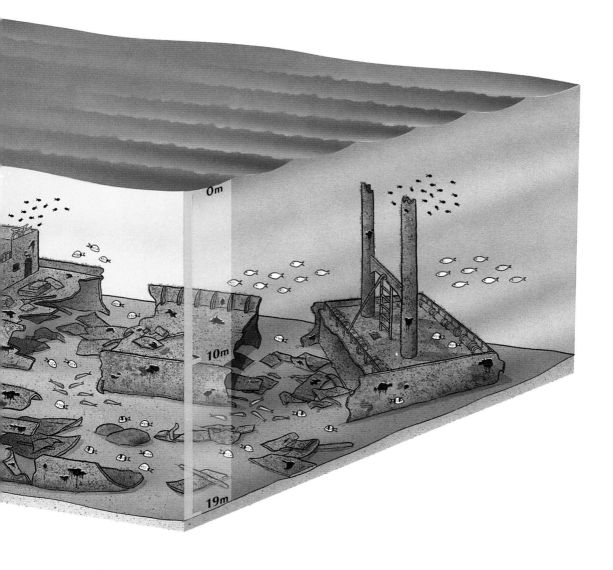

Exactly forty years ago the Roman wreck of Spargi was first discovered, and the first underwater archaeological excavation using modern techniques took place the following year. But many centuries before, in the same waters of the Strait of Bonifacio, an unknown ship sank; it was transporting important cargo: blocks of obsidian, the primary goods of trade for Sardinia at that time, on their way to the northern coasts of the Mediterranean. Who knows how many other boats were caught by the powerful currents of the Strait during ancient times and, buffeted by the waves, shaken by the mistral, and sank without leaving a trace? We know much more about the ships that have sunk during the past two hundred years in the strait that separates Sardinia from Corsica, dividing two seas. Only a few months have passed since the latest in a long series of wrecks, a cargo ship, run aground at Lavezzi and a transport ship foundered on the shoals of Barettini di Fuori. The exact position of many other ships is known, and they are popular with divers, while others have mysteriously disappeared, sucked away by the waves to some unknown part of the Strait. Indeed, it has taken less than 15 years to erase all above-water traces of the wreck of the *Angelika*, which lies west of Punta Marmorata. The last yard that rose out of the water, which made it easy to locate the wreck, was broken by the violence of the waves, and now all the fragments of the cargo ship are scattered among the submerged rocks of the cape. The *Angelika* was a Greek cargo ship, one of the many that ply the waters of the Mediterranean, transporting the most varied materials. The holds of the *Angelika* must have held sugar, grains and various food products, but as usual, whenever a ship sinks, stories of illegal transport abound, with tales of drums full of poisons and any number of other dangerous substances.

The *Angelika* had the misfortune to pass through the Strait on a spring day in 1982 during a storm at sea, and perhaps seeking shelter from the *mistral*, it came too close to the islands that lie across from Punta Marmorata, and ended up on the shoals that make these waters so dangerous. The ship foundered on the rocks and was immediately and irreversibly overcome by the force of the sea, leaving its crew no other choice than to abandon it to its fate and flee to nearby land. The slow and inexorable work of demolition then began, breaking the hull into various pieces and scattering them among the rocks on the sandy sea floor about 20 meters deep.

Of the many wrecks scattered on the floor of the Strait, near Corsica and the La Maddalena Archipelago, the *Angelika* is certainly the most popular with divers, both because of its proximity to large holiday villages that bring swarms of divers to visit it, and because it allows divers to savor the fascination of sunken wrecks in an easy dive, at a shallow depth that provides plenty of time for exploration. The only thing to watch out for is the current, which at times is quite violent, almost as if to remind one that these are indeed the waters of the Strait. The dive begins at the bow, where

A

B

C

A - After the Angelika *sank, its cargo yards emerged about 4 meters above water, making it quite easy to identify. Recently a sea storm broke them off: this is the fate of all ships that lie in shallow waters.*

B - Despite the fact that the wreck has been shattered into various pieces, some parts are still almost intact. The quarter-deck with its stairways, the bridge and the guardrails are easy to explore.

C - The great three-bladed rudder lies on the sandy sea floor, still connected to the axle in the stern fragment. The blades were bent by the violent impact against the shoals.

wreckage, parts of the frame and hard-to-identify fragments are scattered among the rocks.
The prow capstans are recognizable, along with other machinery that form suggestive passageways in some points. From here, following the wreckage, you come to the central masts that supported the yard, now destroyed. The structure was used for loading and unloading goods, and in fact, steel cables, pulleys and hoists still hang from the masts, and the capstans that operated the cables can still be clearly seen.
To the left of the hull, detached from the rest, yet still strangely intact, is the quarter-deck: you can enter the windows and doors for a short visit inside and explore the corridors and connecting stairways between the various levels. On good days, when the water is clear, the light shines in from the portholes and various openings, creating lovely views. From here go to the stern, which is resting on its left side.
The guardrails are still intact, the large mooring bollards are in place, and the large rudder emerges from the sand.
All around is twisted, unrecognizable wreckage.
The drums and barrels that can still be seen among the wreckage were abandoned after the wreck was used as an underwater set during the shooting of a film by Folco Quilici.
The wreck is also interesting due to the organisms that have colonized it, including algae, sponges and many other invertebrates. In various areas of the wreckage are slender colonies of hydrozoans, which flourish in the currents, and on them it is easy to spot violet *Flabellina affinis* and white *Cratena peregrina* that undulate rhythmically.
What is most impressive as you swim through the wreckage of the *Angelika* is the knowledge that this dramatic destruction is entirely the work of the waves: an extraordinary testimony not only to the violence of the forces that shattered the wreck, but above all to their implacability.

D

E

F

G

D - The break-up of the wreck, caused by the impact against the rocks, subsequent storms and fifteen years on the sea floor, does not prevent the identification of its various parts. The engines and the stern are still in good condition.

E - The Angelika *was a cargo ship, and in addition to pulleys and derricks, it was equipped with large capstans for moving goods. All parts of the hull have been covered with algae and sponges.*

F - A door opens darkly from the poop deck, one of the best preserved areas. Even when submerged hulls are in good condition, many dives are necessary in order to reconstruct both an overall picture and the details.

G - The interior of the poop deck is easy to explore. Entering wrecks requires a great deal of experience and special safety measures.

All the photographs concerning the dive on the **Angelika** *are by* **Andrea Ghisotti**

SECCA DI SPARGIOTTELLO

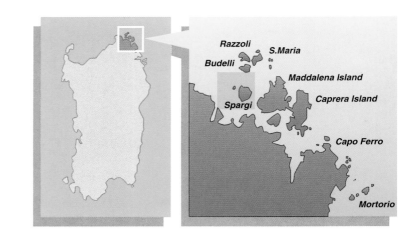

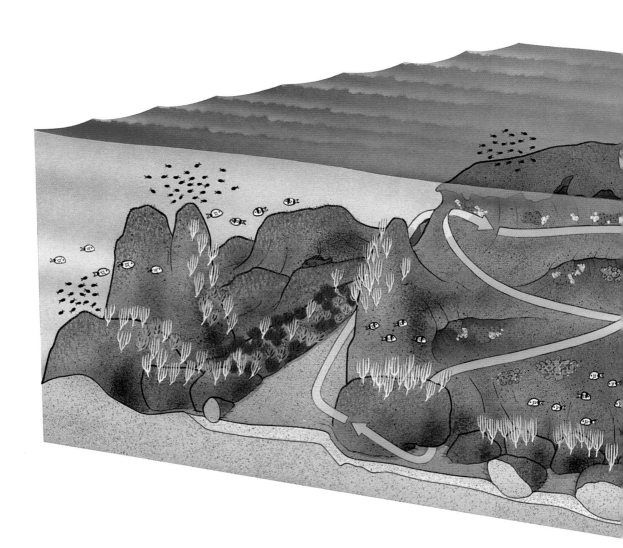

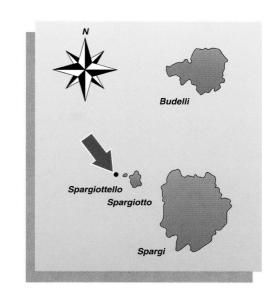

D

To the northwest of Spargi is the reef of Spargiotto, and a little farther west Spargiottello, a few spurs of granite jutting from the surface. Yet a little farther west the light-colored patch of shallow just 3 meters from the surface can easily be seen. It is formed by a large central block which descends gently on one side toward a rockslide that leads to the sand at a depth of about 26 meters. The other side descends vertically onto a channel of sand at a depth of 23 meters that separates it from another vertical area of rock. From the top of the reef descend toward a large mass resting on the seabed, forming a vault. The element that characterizes the entire dive is

immediately evident: on the vertical areas as well as the flat masses, covered with the usual soft carpet of photophilic algae, grow numerous white sea fans (*Eunicella singularis*). Their branches are all straight and elongated, reaching upwards toward the surface, and in many areas form small forests. This is an uncommon situation that changes drastically as you enter the gully that separates these two areas from the shallow. In the less illuminated zone the number of white sea fans drops drastically as yellow ones begin to appear, along with members of the genus *Paramuricea*. Indeed, it is not at all common to see three different

A

B

C

E

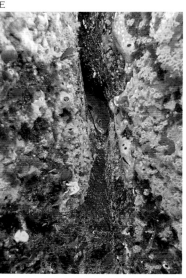

A - To the northwest of the island of Spargi are the shoals of Spargiotto and Spargiottello: farther to the west the shallow stretches out underwater, continuing the form of the emerged islands.

B - A long cornice runs along the upper portion of the shallow, forming cavities and crevices where many organisms hide. The granitic rocks are covered with a thin layer of photophilic algae.

C - The most peculiar aspect of the shallow is the presence of large areas colonized by white sea fans (Eunicella singularis). This species of gorgonian, common on the Sardinian seabeds, is rarely seen in such high concentrations.

D - On the north side of the shallow other sea fans are more numerous and replace the white ones. In some areas three species of gorgonians - yellow, white and red - can be seen together.

E - The granite masses are full of deep fissures. A conger eel hides among the walls covered with golden zoanthids. The fish is waiting for dusk to fall, when it will leave its hiding place to hunt for prey.

F - One of the many rocks colonized by white sea fans: the colonies have upright growth habits with the single branches typical of the species.

G - Morays are also quite common on the shallow. Morays are traditionally considered quite ferocious, probably because their jaws are always gaping wide open. In reality, this behavior merely ensures an adequate flow of water to the gills.

H - Some rocks of the shallow are covered with a carpet of algae from the genus Codium. A scorpionfish, with yellow patches that are mimetic in environmental lighting, can be seen on the algae.

I - Many octopuses build their lairs among the rocks of the shallow. The octopus is a skilled predator, equipped with an extremely effective visual apparatus. Its eyes, which seem so different from ours, nevertheless permit it to see in a very similar manner.

species all together, forming beautiful patterns of color. The more you head north, the greater the number of organisms characteristic of less illuminated areas. The red algae replace the green and brown ones, and large patches of golden zoanthids appear. All around, the seascape is majestic, with the great central bastion surrounded by more fractured rocks. Conger eels and morays peer out of the crevices, and a beautiful grouper swims among the masses that cover the seabed to the north of the shallow, ready to retreat to its lair if you come too close. Large sponges from the genus *Petrosia* have formed a substratum on the walls convenient for colonies of golden zoanthids. This is not a common combination, as normally golden zoanthids colonize sponges from the genus *Axinella*, giving rise to their scientific name, *Parazoanthus axinellae*. Going around the main shallow, return to the side exposed to the light, where the ascent begins. Among the low algae you can see many small red patches of sponges which appear to be moving. In reality the sponge (*Crambe crambe*) entirely covers the shell of a small bivalve (Arca noae, or Noah's ark), which closes up at the sign of any movement. In some areas small rockslides are covered by algae (*Codium*), which have a characteristic hairy appearance. You may also see strange scorpionfish with mimetic coloring with vivid yellow spots. This is a typical case of disruptive mimicry, in which the color breaks up the image of the fish, making it difficult to perceive its outlines. The higher part of the shallow is furrowed by a sequence of low vaults that cross it at various depths. The edge of the projections hosts colonies of hydrozoans, where *Flabellina* nudibranchs graze. Immediately below, a sciophilous environment begins, and among the thin filaments of green algae (*Cladophora*) you will discover a multitude of brightly colored *Thuridilla hopei* sea slugs. Before emerging from the water, your safety stop will take you along the highest projection, where under the little vault you can observe the large variety of organisms that hides here, and the time will pass quickly.

F

G

H
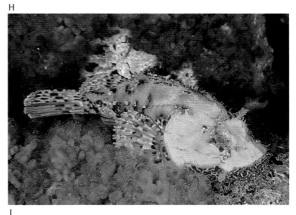

I

SECCA WASHINGTON

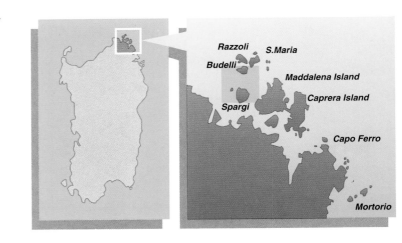

Razzoli S.Maria
Budelli
Maddalena Island
Caprera Island
Spargi
Capo Ferro
Mortorio

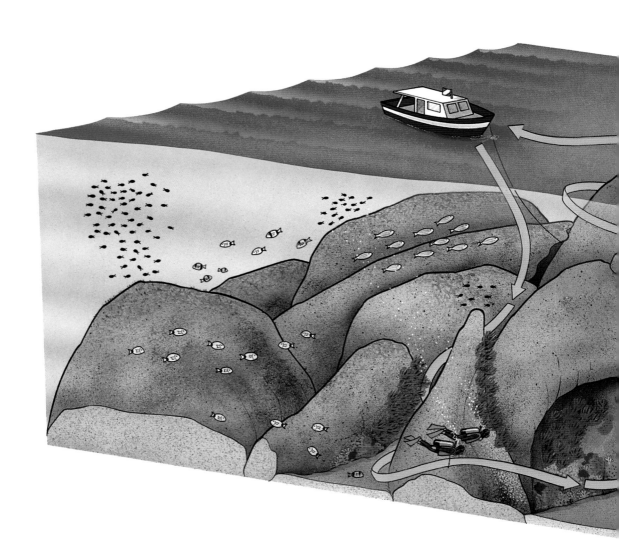

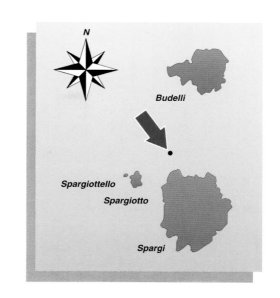

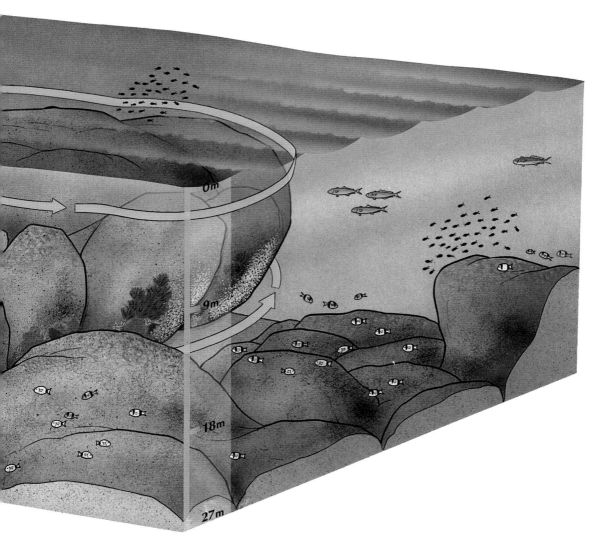

A

B

C

D

E ven from a distance the light patch of this shallow can be seen between the islands of Spargi and Budelli, about one mile north from Punta Zanotto di Spargi. The highest areas are only 6 meters from the surface, and on the rare days when the sea is calm the great granite bastions and the deep fissures carved into them are clearly visible. The shallow is quite large: a wide area of seabed is covered by enormous blocks interspersed with rockslides and smaller masses, often separated by sandy channels swept by the deep currents. It is quite common to find currents on the surface as well, at which point you will have to forego the dive. The current often flows in a different direction from the wind, which makes mooring quite difficult because the boat will tend to move crossways. Despite all this, which makes it necessary to be quite cautious in planning the dive, the fact remains that the shallow offers truly beautiful sights and a large number of possible routes. The picture is completed by

A - North of Spargi is the great underwater complex of Secca Washington. The shallowest rocks can easily be seen from the surface in this crystal clear water.

B - The shallow is formed of enormous blocks of granite furrowed by deep cracks and surrounded by piles of large rounded rocks, resulting in a quite impressive seascape.

C - The red gorgonians are the main attraction of the shallow. They grow on the vertical walls, but also in the passages among the rocky masses. The floor of a tunnel formed by one rock balanced on top of others is covered by sea fans.

E

currents that, starting at a depth of 15 meters, favor the growth of large colonies of sea fans that carpet the northern walls and the channels among the masses. Anchor on the top of the shallow, trying to center over a deep crack where the anchor will not harm the gorgonians. For this reason you should absolutely avoid anchoring north of the largest masses. Descend to the plateau formed by the highest part of the shallow and head north, following a rockslide and the jagged edges of a large

D - Large red sea fans stand out on the walls. Due to their elevated position, the gorgonians create favorable conditions for the growth of other organisms.

E - Large red scorpionfish are common on the rocks of the seabed. This close-up shows the complicated appendages that break up the image of the fish, and its intricate pattern of colors.

granite protuberance. You will come out onto a channel among masses dominated by a pointed spire that rises diagonally toward the surface. The more sheltered side is covered by a carpet of golden zoanthids and red sponges from which the fans of the gorgonians rise. Following the spire toward the seabed, you enter naturally into a passage between the triangular-shaped masses. The red gorgonians grow not only on the walls, but also on the seabed, a clear sign that powerful currents sweep through

beautiful grouper. Sometimes a group of eagle rays seem to fly up from the patches of sand among the masses or from the flat rocky areas. They move away slowly, disturbed by the noise of the bubbles. Going on, the rock becomes sheer, like an enormous belly of granite, and among the golden zoanthids a large quantity of yellow sponges (*Alysina cavernicola*) replaces the gorgonians on the wall.
The structure of the shallow is so imposing that you almost do not

G - The sea fans are often surrounded by carpets of golden zoanthids and colorful sponges. Only the camera flash or a flashlight will reveal this explosion of colors.

F

G

H

F - In certain areas along the vertical wall the sea fans are so thick that they form a small forest.
The gorgonians are all growing in the same direction.

this sort of natural tunnel. Come out onto a channel with a sandy floor surrounded by high rock walls. Following the channel to the left, you will come to the base of enormous blocks that form the central portion of the shallow. The scenery is imposing and the vertical walls in the shadows, seen by the beam of your flashlight, reveal the yellow of the golden zoanthids and the bright red of the gorgonians. In the fissures among the rocks hide large morays, and every so often you may see a

notice the extraordinary variety of organisms that cover the rock. Following the edge of the enormous hulk of rock, spiral up to the main plateau of the shallow, where little clouds of seabreams and schools of salemas move tranquilly about as they search for food among the algae that cover the masses.
The rocks below will still be visible during your brief safety stop before emerging, and as you climb back onto the boat and look at the surrounding islands, it seems a replica of the underwater scene.

H - When the polyps of the colonies of sea fans retract their tentacles, the gorgonian's appearance changes and it seems "thinner." Gorgonians with their polyps expanded are commonly considered to be "in flower," and it is no coincidence that the scientific name for these organisms means animals that look like flowers.

SECCA DEI MONACI

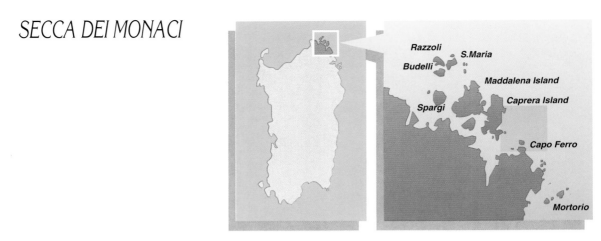

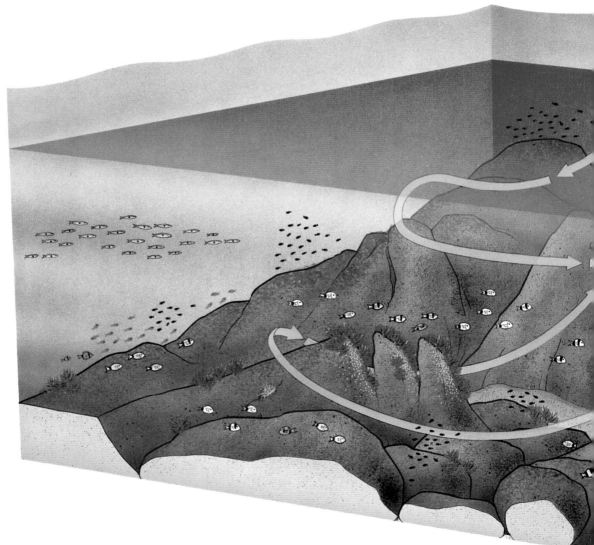

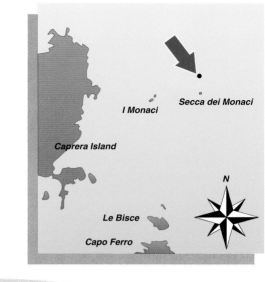

Secca dei Monaci

I Monaci

Caprera Island

Le Bisce

Capo Ferro

N

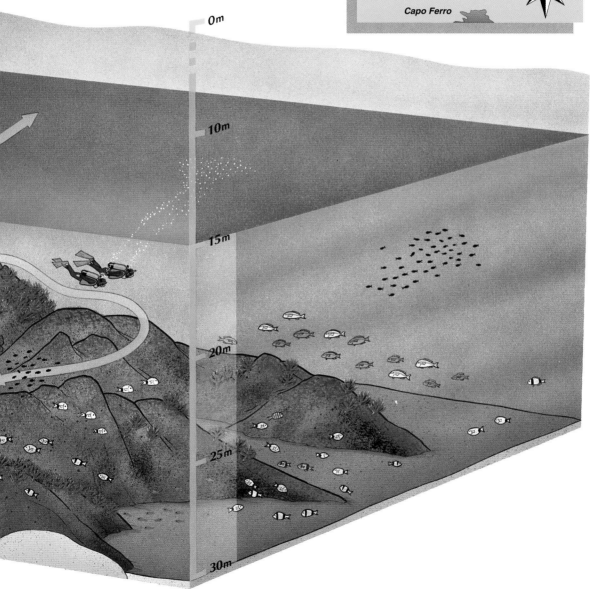

0m

10m

15m

20m

25m

30m

To the east of the island of Caprera a group of granite shoals forms the Secca dei Monaci, the only emerging area in a quite extensive group of shallows. On the largest shoal there is a small lantern, while on the one farther east a beacon marks other shoals that rise almost to the surface. To the north of the signal is the Secca di fuori, which has two shallower points at depths of 13 and 16 meters. When the sea is calm and the water is clear, you can easily see the tops of the reef from the surface. Anchor on the rocks at a depth of 16 meters. The shallow is formed of a group of granite blocks, often quite jagged. The usual cloud of damselfish surrounds the reef,

form spires and narrow clefts. Here there is a true explosion of color: the yellows of the golden zoanthids compete with the red gorgonians which cover entire walls and grow on both sides of the vertical cracks, nearly blocking the way. They are present in great numbers, and their fans are quite large. Dense schools of anthias swim among the sea fans. Although from a distance they appear to be a uniform pinkish red color, from close up males exhibit a complex coloration, with yellow, lilac and pink streaks. Male anthias can also be distinguished by their pectoral and dorsal fins, which are longer than those of the females, and by their generally greater size. As you observe the

and as you descend look around you into the blue depths and you are likely to see schools of dentex and amberjacks. Descend along the slope toward a sandy channel which, at a depth of 27 meters, separates the main rocks from another group of rocky shoals. From the very start the rock is covered with the usual low photophilic algae, but quite soon gorgonians make their appearance, at first sparse and then increasingly thick. In the less exposed areas carpets of golden zoanthids are interrupted by broad areas covered with sponges. They are all *Chondrosia reniformis*, and are more common in dark crevices than in such exposed areas. Passing the sandy channel, the deepest rocks

A - East of Caprera a small lighthouse marks the islet of Monaci, surrounded by a vast area of shallows. A beacon signals a group of almost emerging reefs, and a little to the north is the diving area.

B - The red gorgonians are the main attraction of the shallow. They grow densely here, with large fans on the deeper rocks, especially where the shape of the rocks channels the currents.

C - The concentration of gorgonians is a good indicator of hydrodynamics: probably growth is sparser where there are fewer feeding opportunities.

D - Despite the extraordinarily clear water and the bright light that penetrates to the depths, only the camera flash will bring out the brilliant red of the gorgonians, which otherwise appear to be a uniform dark blue.

gorgonians from below, take a look at the sea above as well, and you will immediately become aware that the water is so clear that you can see the boat moored almost 30 meters above. Many animals live on the gorgonians and take advantage of the favorable position: annelids from the genus *Filograna*, with their complicated masses of little white tubes, are common guests on the sea fans. Going around the spires, you will see a large sea anemone that hosts a whole community of inachus crabs: covered with algae, the inachus live like this, protected by the stinging cells of the sea anemone. Passing the spires, you will come to another rise: here as well, gorgonians and golden

F

E

G

zoanthids cover the areas more exposed to the current. Ascend and come back toward the highest rocks. You will see groups of white and sharpsnout seabreams in search of food: on the top of the masses there are erect colonies of hydrozoans, grazed by various species of nudibranchs, especially *Coryphella*. After reaching the summit of the shallow, before you reemerge there is still time to look around into the blue depths. Often your bubbles will attract amberjacks, while dentex tend to keep their distance. Come up along the mooring line, and as you make your safety stop you will have an excellent overall view of this shallow, heightened by the exceptionally clear water.

H

MORTORIOTTO

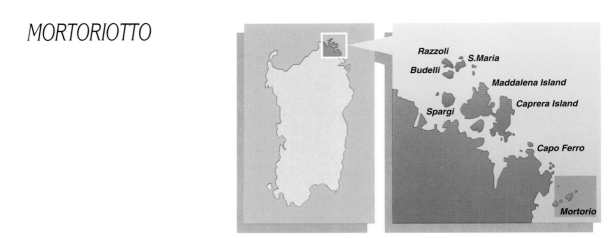

Razzoli
S.Maria
Budelli
Maddalena Island
Spargi
Caprera Island
Capo Ferro
Mortorio

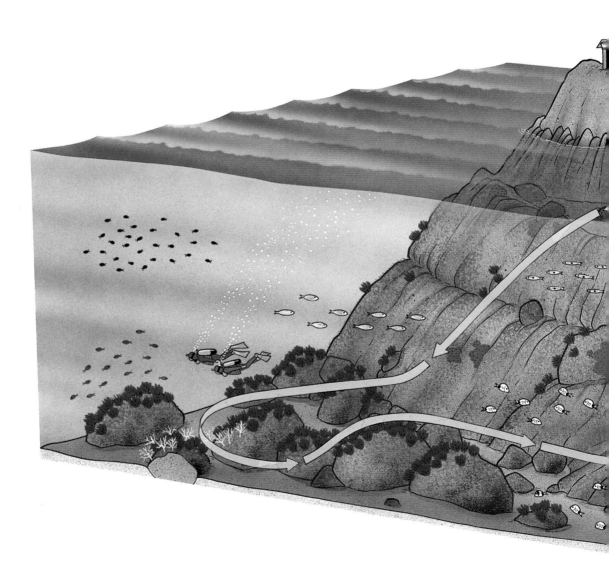

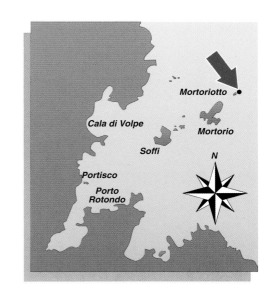

Mortoriotto

Cala di Volpe

Soffi

Mortorio

Portisco

Porto
Rotondo

N

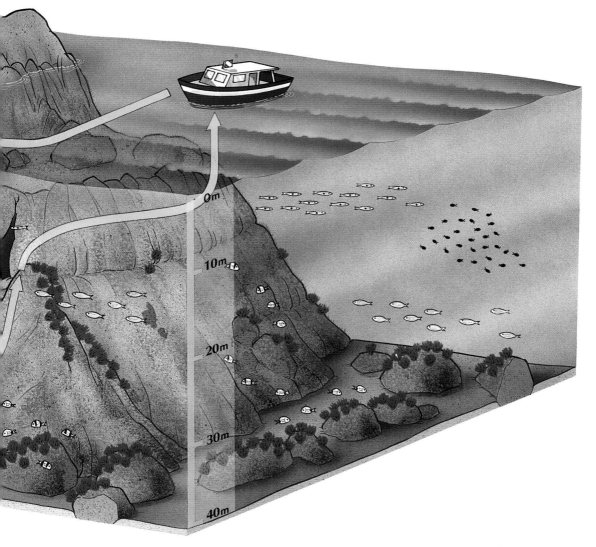

0m

10m

20m

30m

40m

A - Mortoriotto is the outermost shoal in a group of islands and islets. The main ones are Soffi, Camere and Mortorio. There is a signal lamp on Mortoriotto, and the diving area is located on the outer side of the shoal.

B - During the first few meters down, the rocks are covered by large encrusting sponges of various species and colors, all contending for living space.

C - The highlight of the dive is the false black coral (Gerardia savaglia). The yellow Gerardia stands out in the distance on the rocks of the seabed among the sea fans. False black coral is common in deep water, but rare at shallower depths.

D - Many organisms find shelter among the rocks that descend down to the sea floor: a conger eel peeps out of its lair.

E - A hermit crab carries its load of sea anemones: the white filaments released by the sea anemones are stinging and used for defensive purposes. The hermit crab uses this weapon to defend itself, and in exchange provides its guests with mobility and food.

Mortoriotto is the outermost shoal of a group of islands off the Gulf of Cugnana: the other larger ones are Mortorio, Soffi and Camere. The boat moors quite close to the point, directly under the light, and you dive in right along the granite wall that rapidly descends.

The seabed, made of spires and masses, is marked by two drop-offs which terminate on terraces scattered with fallen rocks. Always keeping the slope in sight, head directly to deeper water, where you will find the main attraction of this dive.

Below a depth of 30 meters the sandy floor that drops down to 39 meters is scattered with masses and rocky shoals covered with large red gorgonians, and even from a distance the false black coral is quite visible among the violet blue gorgonians, in a depression between the two rises. Two fair-sized colonies grow here and have colonized part of the skeleton of a gorgonian.

Underwater, false black coral appears yellow, because only the skeleton is black, while the tissue that covers it and within which the polyps are located is light yellow. Its scientific name is *Gerardia savaglia*, and it is only a distant relative of the true black coral of the Indian Ocean.

In many areas of the Mediterranean, in deep water, primarily between 60 to 80 meters, there are sometimes enormous colonies of false black corals. Some of them are over one and a half meters tall. But even the smaller formations at Mortorietto are a sight worth seeing! If there is a bit of current, the polyps of this hexacoral will expand, and they become immediately distinguishable from the yellow gorgonians.

Here, these corals are common at a depth of only 36 meters, almost a record for this colonizing animal. Despite the depth, this seabed is luminous, and the transparency of the water permits a great deal of light to filter down from the surface. Although 36 meters is quite shallow for false black corals, the same cannot be said for divers, and thus you should go back up

E

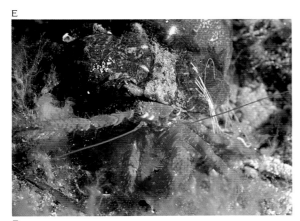

almost a terrace that runs horizontally northward. In the more sheltered zones there are plenty of things to see. It is easy to spot various species of nudibranchs: the most common is a member of the *Eolidiacea* family, *Cratena peregrina*.

Then rise gently toward the surface, coming up toward the outside point of the reef, where your safety stop at a depth of 5 meters can be spent wandering along the wall and exploring among the rocks and crevices.

I - A close-up of the polyps of the black coral easily distinguishes it from gorgonians. Indeed, black coral belongs to a different group of organisms, and is more closely related to sea anemones than to gorgonians.

F

G

H

F - Spiny lobsters are quite common among the rocks of Mortoriotto. Like other crustaceans, their eyes are located at the top of a mobile penduncle in order to increase visual capacity.

G - A small cardinal fish swims in a crevice of the shallow. Like all fish of this genus, it has two light bands across its eyes, which give it a strangely sad expression.

H - A group of tunicates forms a delicate pattern. Tunicates belong to the same group as vertebrates, and thus, despite the great difference in form, from an evolutionary perspective they are our close relatives.

to shallower depths. First swim among the great sea fans that cover the masses: you will find spiny lobsters at the base of the fans among the golden zoanthids. Ascending again, you will reach the slope of a shoal, with a first drop-off among the branches of gorgonians and large red sponges, at a depth of 22 meters.

It is easy to spot morays among the rocks, and the less illuminated areas of the walls are covered with golden zoanthids and red sponges. The sea fans are sparser in the areas more exposed to the currents, and are often colonized with spirographs and *Filograna* nudibranchs.

Continuing the ascent, the gorgonians become even more scattered and finally disappear at a depth of 15 meters, where the algae coverage on the rocks begins to increase, especially in late spring, forming true carpets of glass bell tunicates, ascidians with a chalice-shaped transparent body. At a depth of 12 meters there is another sharp drop-off,

I

BRIEF GUIDE TO THE FLORA AND FAUNA

One of the most oldest activities in the world is observing, classifying and naming things. This becomes more complicated as the number of subjects and observers increases vertiginously, making it necessary to develop universal codes for interpreting and cataloguing that are valid for everyone.

The classification of organisms is based on this fundamental need and on the identification of an entity of reference: the species. All those organisms that have more or less the same morphological characteristics and are able to generate fertile offspring belong to the same species. Everyone seems to agree with this basic concept, developed by Carolus Linnaeus in the 18th century, although the means of determining species, especially in recent times,

have become increasingly refined and at times controversial.

After the basic entity is identified, there are a number of subdivisions that use criteria of affinity in order to group organisms in a manner which makes research more simple. All living beings are classified into 5 kingdoms, very broad categories which are in their turn broken down into increasingly smaller groups. Phylum, class, order, family, genus and finally species are the basic steps of classification. The system is known as binomial classification because all organisms have a name composed of two Latin words: the first indicates the genus, while the second, which always appears in combination, is the species. For example, red coral belongs to the animal kingdom, the *Cnidaria phylum*, the *Anthozoa* class, the *Gorgonacea* order, the *Corallidae* family, the genus *Corallium* and the species *Corallium rubrum*.

Do not be put off by this apparently complicated system, as it actually requires only a bit of practice to master.

In addition, simplifying matters a bit, everything can be summarized within about ten groups.

THE ALGAE
Algae are plants, and as such are capable of producing organic substances through the process of photosynthesis. They have a sometimes complex structure in terms of form which is nevertheless undifferentiated in terms of function: the entire alga is a thallus. They reproduce both sexually and asexually. They are divided into various groups: the most common are the red algae, the brown algae and the green algae. The various groups photosynthesize by using pigments sensitive to various bands of light waves.

THE PHANEROGAMS
These are plants with the same characteristics as land plants, but which are perfectly adapted to the marine environment. They have differentiated organs: roots, stalk, leaves, flowers and fruit. They also reproduce asexually. The most well-known and common is *Posidonia oceanica*, oceanic Neptune grass.

THE SPONGES
These are aquatic animals which for a long time were considered to be plants. Indeed, they have no means of locomotion and have no nervous system. In reality they are animals, because in order to live and grow they feed on other organisms. They can vary greatly in form, but all have a body, supported by spicules of various materials, within which runs a network of channels that lead out into orifices called inhaling and exhaling pores. Using the inhaling pores, the sponges absorb great quantities of water, which is filtered by the cilia that cover the walls of the channels before it is expelled.

THE CNIDARIANS
These animals are more complex than the sponges, for reasons which include the fact that they have a nervous system. The name of the group comes from the presence of stinging cells (from the

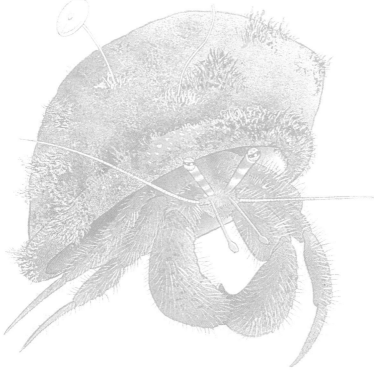

Greek *cnidè*) in the bodies of these organisms. They have two fundamental forms: polyp and medusan. Polyp forms live attached to the sea floor, while the medusan varieties live freely among the plankton. They can be single or colonial, and often the colonies of polyps are supported by skeletons of various consistencies. They reproduce both sexually and by fission. Jellyfish, sea anemones, stony corals, gorgonians and corals belong to this group.

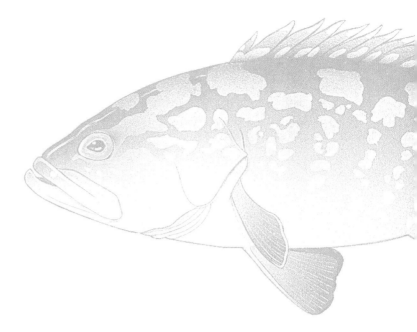

THE WORMS

This generic and not very scientific name actually includes many different types of animals, with quite different forms and ways of life. The most numerous group is that of the annelids, with bodies formed of many segments, all equal except for the first and the last. The most well-known annelids are the spirographs. Another group is the platyhelminths, flat worms with a leaf-shaped body which is often brightly colored. The echiuridae have yet a different form, and make up an extremely small family worldwide.

THE MOLLUSKS

These animals have soft bodies with no supporting structures, and are generally protected by a shell which may be in one, two or eight parts. They have well-developed systems and reproduce sexually, with numerous hermaphrodite species. This is the group of complex marine organisms with the largest number of known species, for reasons which include the fact that their shells are used as goods of exchange and are gathered by collectors, thus contributing to knowledge about them. Moreover, many species are an integral part of the human diet, and they are fished and cultivated. Cowries, nudibranchs, mussels and octopuses are mollusks.

THE CRUSTACEANS

These belong to the *phylum* of arthropods, which also include insects. They are animals with a body protected by a rigid carapace, or armor, flexible at the joints and equipped with a large number of appendages. In addition to their limbs, these animals have complex mouth apparatuses, sensory bristles and antennae. They reproduce sexually, and many species are hermaphrodites. They are present in all marine environments, and the planktonic component is an extremely important link in the food chain. Lobsters, crabs and shrimp belong to this group.

THE BRYOZOANS

These are strange colonial animals characterized by a sort of tuft of tentacles in the form of a horseshoe that serves to collect food. The colony is formed by a calcareous or parchment-like support, full of niches which host the individual members of the colony, all of which are connected to each other. Within the colony the various individuals may have different specialized functions. The form of the colony may be branched or else encrusting if on hard substrata.

THE ECHINODERMS

This is a group of animals with a pentamerous, radially symmetrical form. Sea urchins, starfish, red stars, sea cucumbers and crinoids belong to this group. A common element is the presence of a hard skeleton which is coherent and external in sea urchins and comprised of structures distributed throughout the body in the other groups. Another typical feature is spines, which are evident in sea urchins. All have a complex system of locomotion consisting of pedicles operated by a hydraulic system known as the aquiferous system. They reproduce sexually and live on the sea floor.

THE CHORDATES

Vertebrates, including human beings, belong to this group. The element which animals in this group have in common is the presence, at some point in their lives, of a sort of backbone similar to our spinal cord. Tunicates have it only during the larval stage, and adults look nothing at all like other vertebrates. Fish are typically aquatic vertebrates which breathe by means of gills. They have a hydrodynamic shape and are often covered with scales, with specialized structures for locomotion: their fins. They reproduce sexually and live in the water, or else in close contact with the sea floor.

ALGAE

Umbrella weed - *Acetabularia mediterranea*

Although this is classified as a green alga, it is white in colour and only rarely has a greenish cast. Its little umbrella form makes it unmistakable: the disc at the end of the thin stalk is marked by radiating furrows. This is an alga typical of well-illuminated areas near the surface with a high level of sedimentation. Sometimes it forms true meadows and covers the entire sea floor.

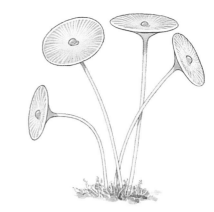

Udotea - *Udotea petiolata*

This is a green alga typical of dimly lighted areas and is usually associated with other algae typical of precoralligenous environments. It characteristically has a thin peduncle attached to the rock, with fan-shaped fronds. It is often colonized by small invertebrates, especially worms from the Polychaeta class.

Leafy caulerpa - *Caulerpa prolifera*

This is a green alga which colonizes illuminated detrital areas. The thallus consists of a stolon anchored to the sea floor by small branches, from which leaf-shaped fronds grow. It can adhere to mobile seabeds in calm waters, where it creates conditions favorable for the growth of *Cymodocea* or *Posidonia*.

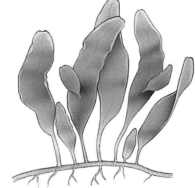

Purse codium - *Codium bursa*

This is the most common species of a genus of green algae which all have a velvety external appearance and a hollow body. It is most common in well-illuminated areas, and when it becomes large the central portion collapses, forming the typical depression. It is often found on the beach at low tide.

Sea cactus - *Halimeda tuna*

The form of the thallus with rounded articulation gives it the appearance of a small prickly pear cactus. It is typical of dimly illuminated areas and is quite common on vertical walls. The thallus has a high content of calcium carbonate, which is quite evident during the reproduction period, when the entire living part of the alga transforms into little spores (sporangia) concentrated at the edge of each segment.

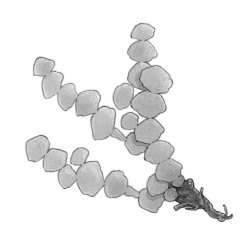

Marine peacock's tail - *Padina pavonica*

This is a brown alga, but the high calcium carbonate content in the thallus gives it a characteristic white colour. Its fan-shaped form gives it the common name of peacock's tail. It is quite common in areas with strong illumination, where it forms small "bushes." It also grows well in warm waters where the hydrodynamics are not overly strong.

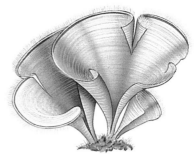

Forked ribbon - *Dictyota dichotoma*

This is a brown alga, although it is usually more green in colour. It has an extremely branching form: the ribbon-shaped thallus is divided into two at each branching point (thus the description dichotoma, or dichotomous). It is quite common on rocks in relatively calm areas. During its period of greatest growth it may take on beautiful iridescent dark blue or azure colours.

Common sargassum - *Sargassum vulgare*

This is a brown alga typical of exposed areas. It has an extremely branched thallus that grows erect. At the base of the branches it has small round cysts (aerocysts) which float and help to keep the thallus erect. In Sardinia it is quite common on the summit of the reefs and on the more exposed wreckage of sunken ships.

False gorgon- *Sphaerococcus coronopifolius*

This is also known as gorgonian alga due to its quite branched appearance and dark red colour. It is a red alga typical of poorly illuminated areas, and can easily be found under rocky masses and in dark crevices where there is a slight current. Dozens of small mollusks can often be found feeding on its thallus.

Peysonellia - *Peyssonellia squamaria*

A red alga with a soft thallus in the form of a rounded lamina. It grows in poorly illuminated areas and is a typical component of precoralligenous and coralligenous zones. Sometimes it takes on a fluorescent orange colour which is only visible underwater. It is common on vertical walls, sometimes underneath green algae, and in dark areas where it covers concretions formed by other calcareous red algae.

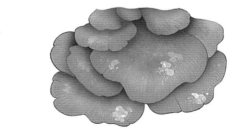

Laminar rockweed - *Pseudolithophyllum expansum*

This is a typical "building" alga: indeed, except for the reddish purple superficial portion, its body, sometimes in a laminar form and rounded with an undulating edge, contains calcium carbonate that binds the thalli of the alga together, and even the other organisms that settle around it. It is the most common member of coralligenous environments.

PLANTS

Eel grass - *Cymodocea nodosa*

This is one of the five species of phanerogams which grow in the Mediterranean. It is typical of detrital seabeds, where it looks like blades of grass. Sometimes it forms true meadows, within which can be found a large quantity of algae and other organisms. It flowers in the spring, with an orange, characteristically three-lobed flower.

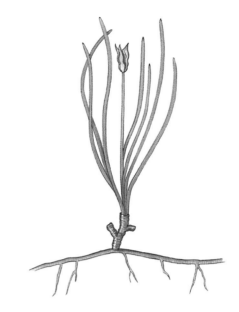

Neptune grass - *Posidonia oceanica*

This is the classic phanerogam of the Mediterranean, and its meadows run along the entire perimeter of Sardinia. In autumn the flowers can be seen on the upper meadows, while the fruits can be found on the beach in late winter. Neptune grass is a species of extraordinary ecological importance, and every part of the plant forms environments where an enormous quantity of other plant and animal species find refuge.

SPONGES

Yellow clathrina - *Clathrina clathrus*

This yellow sponge is extremely common in poorly illuminated areas. Its body, which contains calcareous spicules, looks like a network of little, more or less swollen tubes which are soft to the touch. The oscula, which the sponge uses to expel the water that circulates within its body, are located at the tip of the largest little tubes. It reproduces sexually.

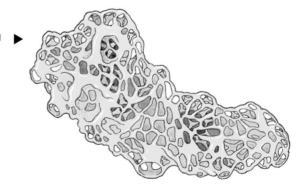

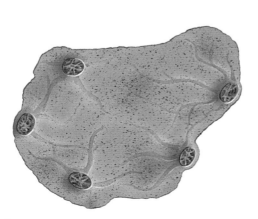

Orange encrusting sponge - *Spirastrella cunctatrix*

This is an extremely common sponge which grows by expanding on rocky walls or by enveloping other organisms. It is bright orange, and the channels which run through its body and lead to the oscula can be seen on its surface. It often occupies large surfaces in poorly illuminated areas.

Common antlers sponge - *Axinella sp.*

The axinellae are a genus of sponges quite common in all environments. They are generally yellow or orange-yellow in colour. The various species have different forms: *A. polipoides* has elongated branches and is typical of rocky seabeds with a high level of sedimentation. *A. verrucosa* has thick cylindrical branches and is common at shallow depths.

Pink tube sponge - *Haliclona mediterranea*

This sponge has an unmistakable form, with elongated tubes that terminate in wide oscula, and a distinctive pink-lilac colour. It is common on shaded walls, along with stony corals and golden zoanthids. Sometimes it can be found in large colonies on the upper areas of sunken ships.

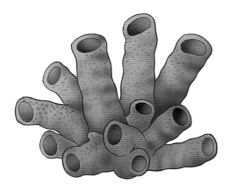

Stony sponge - *Petrosia ficiformis*

This is an extremely common sponge which in illuminated areas takes on its characteristic pale red colour. The colour is due to the presence of photosynthetic cyanobacteria which live symbiotically with the tissues of the sponge. In fact, in poorly illuminated areas the sponge appears white due to the absence of these cyanobacteria. It is commonly associated with the dotted sea slug *Discodoris atromaculata*, which feeds on the tissues of the sponge.

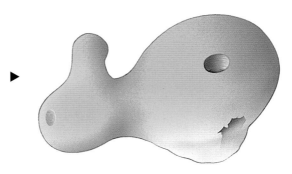

Greek bath sponge - *Spongia officianalis*

This is the classic bathtub sponge. Its body is extremely elastic due to the presence of very flexible spicules of spongin. Its outer appearance is globular, with sparse oscula, and it is a mouse grey colour. It is common in caves and poorly illuminated areas even at extremely shallow depths, but it can also be found at depths of up to 40 metres in areas with a fair degree of hydrodynamics.

Gold sponge - *Aplysina aerophoba*

Yellow in colour, it has a body which consists of a globular base from which branches and additional smaller branchlets extend. The oscula are located at the tips of the branches. It is common on rocky seabeds with photofilic algae, at the entrance to caverns and in meadows of Neptune grass. It is often associated with a pleurobranchomorphous mollusk, *Tylodina perversa*, which feeds on the tissues of the sponge and often spends its entire life on it.

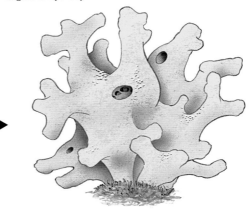

CNIDARIANS

Tree hydroid - *Eudendrium sp.*

These are colonial organisms from the Hydrozoan class. The colonies have an arborescent form with irregular branches. At the ends of the branches are small polyps with 30 tentacles, at the tips of which there are stinging cells which are used to capture food. The mouth is located in the center of the circle of tentacles and leads to the inner cavity. Many nudibranchs from the genera *Flabellina*, *Cratena*, *Eubranchus*, etc. prey upon it.

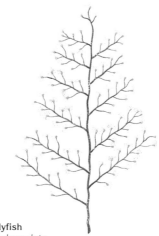

Fried egg jellyfish
Cothyloriza tuberculata

This is an extremely common jellyfish, especially in late summer. It has a brown umbrella with a diameter smaller than the group of tentacles. It has eight arms branched into many small tentacles, which terminate in white or violet disks. It can swim weakly by moving the edge of its umbrella. It has no stinging effect on humans and often hosts small horse-mackerel or crabs, which use it as a shelter.

Luminescent jellyfish - *Pelagia noctiluca*

This is the classic stinging jellyfish, great numbers of which sometimes occupy entire stretches of the sea. Its umbrella is semi-spherical with a ragged edge. It has four arms, but its thin stinging tentacles branch off from the edge of the umbrella and can be dozens of centimetres long. Contact with the tentacles causes a strong burning sensation.

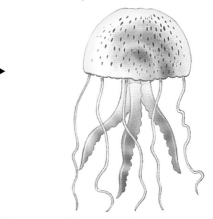

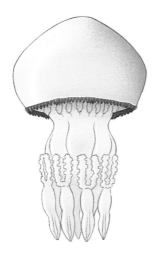

Rhizostome - *Rhizostoma pulmo*

This is the largest jellyfish in the Mediterranean and can reach up to 60 cm in diameter. It is a translucent white, and the edges of the umbrella are violet. It has a leathery consistency and is not very stinging to humans. The eight arms are quite evident and are very ragged on the initial portion. It often hosts horse-mackerel or crustaceans, which take shelter in its umbrella or arms.

Red coral - *Corallium rubrum*

This is the red coral used in jewelry. It is a colonial animal comprised of a hard red skeleton made of calcium carbonate, enveloped in a sort of skin (coenosarc) within which the polyps lie. The white polyps have eight pinnate tentacles and can be extended or withdrawn. The coral prefers half-lit caves for its habitat, but can be found in many other areas with poor illumination, a constant level of salinity and low hydrodynamics.

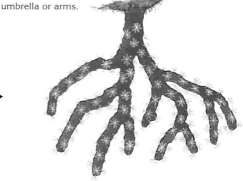

Red sea fan - *Paramuricea clavata*

This is the classic red gorgonian. It forms branching fans up to one metre high, generally on a single level. Like coral, it is a colonial animal, but has a flexible horny skeleton. Its polyps are red. A bi-coloured variety exists in which the branches range from red to yellow and are rarely completely yellow. The bi-coloured colonies are quite localized.

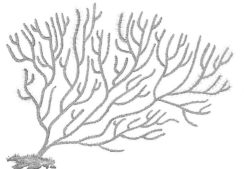

Yellow sea fan - *Eunicella cavolinii*

This is the yellow gorgonian, quite common at even shallow depths. It lives in areas with poor illumination and a fair level of hydrodynamics. It is generally quite branching and has a very flexible skeleton. It often hosts a small gastropod mollusk, *Neosimnia spelta*, which feeds on the polyps of the gorgonian. The mantle that covers the mollusk's shell is quite mimetic, making it difficult to distinguish from the tissues of the gorgonians.

White sea fan - *Eunicella singularis*

This is a white gorgonian with elongated threadlike branches, generally turned upwards. Under special circumstances it will form true carpets on both rocky and detrital seabeds. When it lives in well-illuminated areas, it has microscopic symbiotic algae in its tissues that give it a greenish colour. The polyps are always slightly darker.

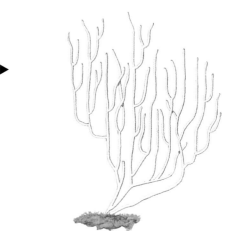

Dead man's finger - *Alcyonium palmatum*

This is a colonial animal that belongs to the same group as corals and gorgonians, but unlike these does not have a hard skeleton, and is instead supported by scattered spicules within the body of the colony. It is red or pinkish in colour and has small white polyps with eight pinnate tentacles. The colony develops on a primary stele with stumpy branches.

Encrusting alcionarian - *Parerythopodium coralloides*

This is a colonial alcyonacea similar to the soft corals of tropical seas. The colony's connective tissue is red, while the polyps are yellow with white tentacles. Normally it grows on the skeletons of gorgonians or on other substrata in favorable positions exposed to the currents. Sometimes it colonizes abandoned nets or the wreckage of sunken ships.

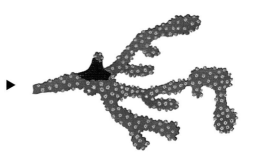

Golden anemone - *Condylactis aurantiaca*

This is a sea anemone typical of sandy or detrital mobile seabeds. It is solitary, with the colony dug into the sediment, and its exposed tentacles open radially. The approximately 100 tentacles are white with lilac-coloured tips. It often hosts symbiotic shrimp from the genus Periclemenes.

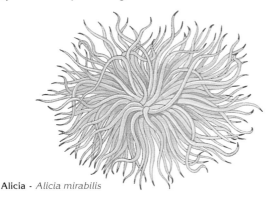

Snakelocks anemone - *Anemonia sulcata*

With about 200 tentacles, this is the largest sea anemone in the Mediterranean. Normally the colony is hidden among the rocks, with only the tentacles visible: they are greenish with violet-lilac tips. It lives in well-illuminated environments, and symbiotic algae are present in its tentacles. Some crustaceans (*Inachus* and *Pilumnus*) and fish (*Gobius bucchichi*) live in contact with the column or among the tentacles.

Alicia - *Alicia mirabilis*

This is the most beautiful and stinging sea anemone in the Mediterranean. By day it is a mass covered with tubercles, while by night it distends its column and tentacles and can reach a length of one and a half metres. The tubercles are located on the extended column, while the extremely long tentacles are often twisted spiral-fashion and are actively used to capture small prey.

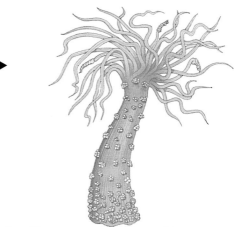

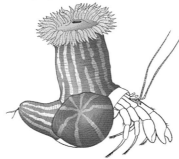

Parasitic anemone - *Calliactis parasitica*

This is a sea anemone which normally lives in symbiosis with the hermit crab *Dardanus arrosor*. It has a stubby brown column with light vertical stripes. Its tentacles are short and quite numerous (over 500). If disturbed, it issues long, thin, white or lilac-coloured, extremely stinging filaments from the base of the column.

Cladocora - *Cladocora caespitosa*

This is the Mediterranean stony coral most similar to tropical corals. It is a colonial animal, and the form of the colony varies depending on environmental conditions. It most commonly appears as a little cushion with individual corals growing quite close to each other. Usually the only visible part is the end portion of the calcareous skeleton with its cylindrical branches, from which the polyp protrudes with its short, transparent tentacles.

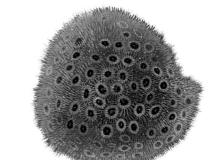

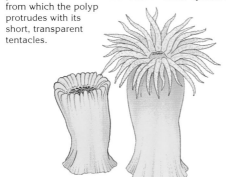

Yellow solitary coral - *Leptosammia pruvoti*

This is a typical stony coral in dimly-illuminated areas, with a hard, lemon yellow skeleton with polyps of the same colour. The tentacles are rough and surround the always visible mouth. This is a solitary species which nevertheless often covers broad areas of the substratum.

Yellow encrusting anemone - *Gerardia savaglia*

This is the false black coral of the Mediterranean, and is only distantly related to true tropical coral. The only black portion is the hard skeleton with the consistency of ebony: the living portion and the polyps are a light yellow colour. It can easily be distinguished from gorgonians due to the large size of its polyps, which clearly extend from the branches.

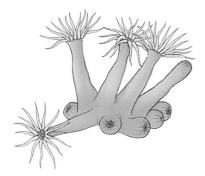

Bushy anemone - *Parazoanthus axinellae*

Commonly known as the golden zoanthid, this is a colonial animal formed of many individual polyps joined together by a common connective tissue. It is orange yellow in colour and often covers large, poorly illuminated walls fully exposed to the currents. It is easily distinguished from *Leptosammia* by the absence of a skeleton and its smooth tentacles.

Cylinder anemone - *Cerianthus membranaceus*

Similar to sea anemones, the tube dwelling anemone is nevertheless easily distinguished by its two principal characteristics: it has two groups of tentacles, with the outer ones longer than the inner ones, and a retractile body with a membranous sheath. It has more than 200 tentacles, and their colour varies greatly, from white to dark brown to violet. This animal is typical of areas with a high degree of sedimentation, such as caves or Neptune grass meadows.

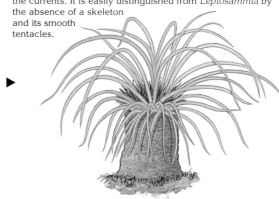

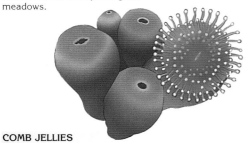

Jewel anemone - *Corynactis viridis*

Although it belongs to another order, the Corallimorpharia, it is quite similar to sea anemones, but does not exceed one centimetre in diameter. It is called the jewel anemone due to its small size and the presence of about a hundred short tentacles that end in a spherical swelling. It can take on quite diverse colours, from lime green to lilac to orange. Usually colonial, it is an animal typical of areas with strong hydrodynamics.

COMB JELLIES

Venus' girdle - *Cestus veneris*

A planktonic animal, the Venus' girdle has a transparent, ribbon-shaped body with rounded extremities. Rows of tiny, continuously vibrating tentacles run across the edge of the body and its middle. The mouth is in the center of the body and receives food captured and transported by the continuous movement of the tentacles. With a body consisting almost entirely of water, it is an extremely fragile animal.

Comb jelly - *Beroe ovata*

The helmet combjelly has a body shaped like a transparent barrel, traversed by several longitudinal rows of vibrating cilia, known as combs, in which the continuous movement of the little tentacles creates a phenomenon of light diffraction. The mouth is in the lower part of the body and receives food carried in along the combs. It can be highly bioluminescent.

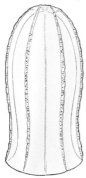

WORMS

Pink flatworm - *Prosthecaereus giesbrechtii*

This is a platyhelminthe, a very common, brightly coloured flatworm. White and lilac streaks run across its body.
Two small "ears" on the front end serve as sensory organs. Its mouth is located in the center of the lower portion of the body. It moves by sliding along the seabed using continuously moving cilia located on its underside. It is an active predator of ascidians and mollusks.

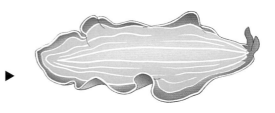

Spiral tube worm - *Sabella spallanzani*

This is the classic spirograph. Its body is protected inside a long tube with a parchment-like texture, from which the large branchial tuft projects. The tuft has respiratory and food gathering functions, and may vary greatly in colour, from dark striped brown to white. The animal is quite sensitive to movement and changes in light, and often retracts.

Red tubicolous worm - *Serpula vermicularis*

This is a spirograph typical of poorly illuminated areas. It has a calcareous tube and a branchial tuft with two pink volutes. A pedunculated operculum is located among the branchiae and is used by the worm to retreat and close the entrance to the tube. It is quite sensitive to the movement of the water that surrounds it and will retract rapidly.

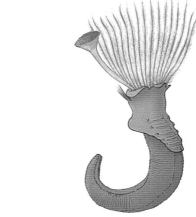

Smooth calcareous worm - *Protula tubularia*

It has a fully visible, calcareous white tube: the bilobate branchial tuft appears more unkempt that those of other spirographs, and usually it is white, although there are red and orange varieties. This animal is quite common in various environments, provided there is adequate sedimentation.

Coral worm - *Filograna implexa*

It looks like a disorderly group of little white tubes that form a rounded mass. It consists of many small individuals with bilobate branchial tufts which are usually transparent, but may be yellow or orange. These annelids live in poorly illuminated environments exposed to currents. They often grow among the branches of gorgonians.

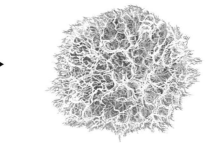

Bonellia - *Bonellia viridis*

It is a member of the Echiuroidea phylum. It has a bean-shaped body with a long proboscis that forks at the end.
It is common in poorly illuminated areas. Sexual dimorphism is quite accentuated: in fact, the male is quite small and lives as a parasite on the body of the female. The determination of sex is also quite unusual: the larvae become male if they come into contact with a female, while they will develop into females if they fall to the seabed in an area with no females.

MOLLUSKS

Chiton - *Chiton olivaceus*

It has an oval shell composed of 8 jointed pieces, from which the edge of the mantle protrudes. The shell may be many different colours, from olive grey to red to sky blue. It lives under rocks, where it feeds by scraping encrusting algae.

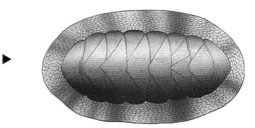

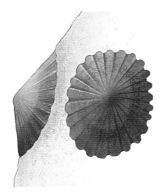

Rayed mediterranean limpet e Ferrous limpet
Patella caerulea and *P. ferruginea*

Limpets have a conical-shaped shell and live at about sea level, attached to the rock by a sturdy foot. They feed on algae which they scrape from the rock with a radula, a sort of toothed tongue. *Patella caerulea* has a flattish shell with no ribbing, while *P. ferruginea* is a larger species that has a high shell with pronounced ribbing. It has become a rare species in Sardinia.

Rough turbo - *Astrea rugosa*

It has a beautiful, spiral-shaped shell with a characteristic operculum used to close the opening. The operculum is orange on the outside, while inside it is light-coloured with a spiral design. Commonly known as the rough turbo, it is used to make pendants. *Astrea rugosa* lives by grazing on algae, and often it is difficult to identify because the shell is covered by a soft layer of algae that can be confused with its surroundings.

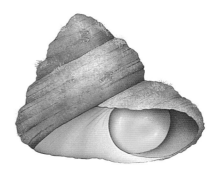

Giant wormshell - *Vermetus arenarius*

It has a tube-shaped shell which assumes a spiral shape only during its developmental stage. Attached to the rocks, this mollusk has a quite unique manner of feeding. It issues a filament of mucous which is carried by the current and attaches to protuberances on the sea floor. The mucous acts as a net that collects suspended organic particles. The filament is withdrawn periodically and the material captured is ingested.

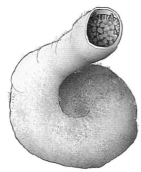

Mediterranean cowrie - *Luria lurida*

This is the most common cowrie in the Mediterranean. Its shell is normally covered by its mantle and remains quite shiny. It is common in dark areas and is nocturnal. It feeds on sponges, which it scrapes with its radula. Considered rare, in reality it is quite common, only difficult to see because it is quite reclusive and mimetic.

Yellow tylodina - *Tylodina perversa*

This is a small sea slug with a cone-shaped shell that does not entirely cover its body. It is bright yellow, with two tentacles on its head, with a large gill on the right side of its body. It feeds exclusively on the sponge *Aplysina aerophoba*, on which it spends most of its life.

Thuridilla - *Thuridilla hopei*

This sea slug is a member of the Sacoglossa order. It has no shell. Its body is elongated, and the upper portion has two lobes which are usually closed. It has two large tentacles on its head. It is quite colourful and feeds on algae, which it grazes primarily in shallow waters.

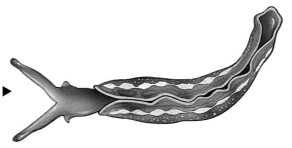

Giant doris - *Hypselodoris valenciennesi*

This is one of the larger nudibranchs, and some individuals in fact reach a length of 20 centimetres. It has an elongated body with two retractile rhinophores in the front and a branchial tuft which is also retractile on the back portion, which ends in a pointed tail. It can vary greatly in colour, with a light body often marked by azure blue tones covered with yellow streaks and spots.

Dotted sea slug - *Discodoris atromaculata*

This is one of the most common nudibranchs and is quite frequent in Sardinia. It is known as the dotted sea slug due to its characteristic colouring, white with dark spots which are larger in the central portion of its oval-shaped body. Its front portion has two white rhinophores and the branchial tuft. It is a predator specialized in the sponge *Petrosia ficiformis*.

Pink flabellina - *Flabellina affinis*

A quite common nudibranch with a garish violet colour, it lives clinging to colonies of hydrozoans, on which polyps it preys. Its body is covered with elongated appendages traversed by a clear filament which is visible against the light. It may be confused with its relative *Flabellina ischitana*, which is distinguished by the red filaments within its appendages, or with *Coryphella pedata*, which is distinguished by its annular rhinophores.

Hervia - *Cratena peregrina*

This is the most common nudibranch in Sardinia, and can be seen during almost every dive. It has a white body covered with long orange-violet appendages. Its front portion has two clear orange spots between the white oral tentacles and orange rhinophores. It feeds on hydrozoans, on which colonies it also lays its eggs with their tangled white filaments.

Noble pen shell - *Pinna nobilis*

This is the largest bivalve in the Mediterranean, and mature specimens about 20 years old can reach one metre in length. It lives in detrital environments and Neptune grass meadows, where it is often colonized by other organisms such as sponges, hydrozoans and ascidians. It hosts symbiotic shrimp and crabs. It is a highly protected species and is increasingly rare along the coast of Sardinia.

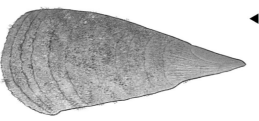

Winged shell - *Pteria hirundo*

Its shell is wing-shaped, and it normally lives in environments exposed to currents. It often lives on colonies of sea fans or other gorgonians, taking advantage of the favorable position. This bivalve clings to the branches of its host by means of a byssus, a group of sturdy filaments which solidify upon contact with water.

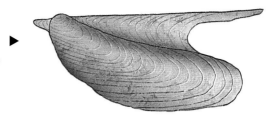

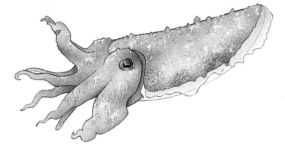

Common cuttlefish - *Sepia officinalis*

This is a cephalopod which retains a residual shell: the cuttlebone. It has eight short tentacles and two longer ones which are used to capture its prey. The cuttlefish is quite mimetic and can rapidly change colour. Its eggs are round with a pointed bottom, and hatch into fully formed little cuttlefish.

Common octopus - *Octopus vulgaris*

The octopus is a cephalopod with eight arms, and is capable of camouflaging itself by changing both the colour and form of its body. It is an extremely intelligent animal, and laboratory experiments have shown that it is capable of learning by observing others. After mating, the female lays her eggs in a cavity and guards them without eating until they hatch: for this reason females often die after reproduction.

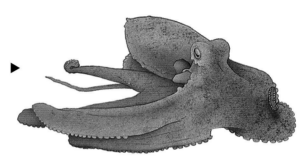

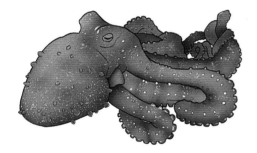

White spotted octopus - *Octopus macropus*

Known as the white spotted octopus, it has longer tentacles than the common octopus and is almost exclusively nocturnal. It can easily be distinguished by its reddish brown colour with quite visible white spots over its entire body. Like the common octopus, it lives in all environments down to depths of about 100 metres.

CRUSTACEANS

Barnacle - *Balanus perforatus*

This is commonly known as the acorn barnacle. It lives within a conical shell firmly anchored to the rocks or artificial substrata, with its upper portion closed by four mobile plates. Within its shell, the animal lives lying on its "back," and feeds by capturing suspended particles through its cirri, modified claws, which are continuously extended and retracted in and out of the shell.

Mediterranean cleaner shrimp - *Stenopus spinosus*

Known as the banded shrimp, it lives exclusively in dark caves. Its body is orange yellow and its third pair of claws, which are quite long, end in pincers. The long white antennae on its head are used to communicate with its "customers," the large fish such as groupers and amberjacks which it cleans.

Narval shrimp - *Pesionika narval*

This shrimp can be found in dark caves, where it lives in groups of dozens of individuals. It has an extremely long, toothed front rostrum, long white antennae and an elongated body streaked with red and white. It is commonly found on sandy seabeds down to great depths, even beyond 800 metres.

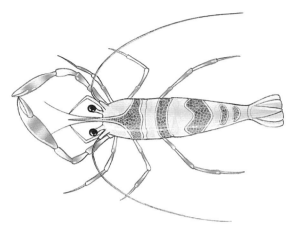

Periclimenes - *Periclemenes amethysteus*

This is also known as the anemone shrimp. It has an almost completely transparent body with some pink-coloured areas. It often lives in symbiosis with the sea anemones *Codylactis aurantiaca* and *Cribrinopsis crassa*. There are other similar species, such as *P. sagittifer*, which has violet spots and a pronounced V-shaped mark on the abdomen.

Lobster - *Homarus gammarus*

Unlike the spiny lobster, this lobster has two large asymmetrical claws. It is a deep yellow colour with blue spots, while its antennae are red. It lives in caves and cavities, from which it comes out at night to hunt. It can become quite large, and is usually sedentary and territorial.

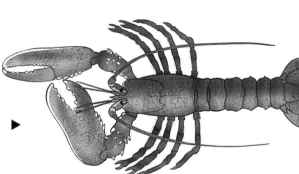

Common spiny lobster - *Palinurus elephas*

The spiny lobster lives on rocky seabeds in coralligenous areas, but can also be found in rocky areas among meadows of Neptune grass. It has long antennae with a sensory function, no claws, and it generally feeds on dead animals. It is commonly fished.

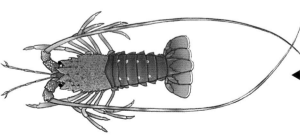

Mediterranean locust lobster - *Scyllarides latus*

The squill or locust lobster is common in dark areas. Its antennae are modified into two wide, jointed plates. A large red spot similar to an eye can be seen on its abdomen, directly behind its shell. In late spring it comes to the surface to deposit its eggs. It is considered an increasingly rare species and is in any event localized. The small locust lobster (*Scyllarus arctus*) is a similar but smaller species.

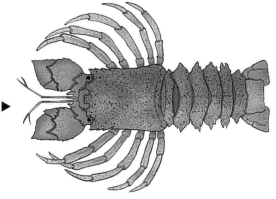

Ridged claw hermit crab - *Dardanus arrosor*

This is the classic hermit crab, bright red with two sturdy claws. Like all hermit crabs, it has a soft abdomen which it protects within shells or other suitable containers. Usually a number of sea anemones (*Calliactis parasitica*) can be found on its shell, with which it lives symbiotically. The sea anemones protect the hermit crab, while the anemones enjoy better feeding opportunities.

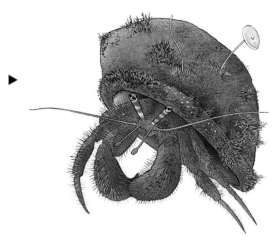

Spiny squat-lobster - *Galathea strigosa*

Although it does not have a soft abdomen, it belongs to the same group as the hermit crabs. It is a beautiful red-orange colour with azure blue streaks, and lives exclusively in dark cracks, from which it comes out at night to hunt. It has two well-developed pincers and long antennae on its head. It moves quite quickly in sudden jerks.

Sleepy crab - *Dromia personata*

This is also known as the porter crab because, especially when young, it breaks off a piece of sponge from the wall and uses it to cover itself, carrying it along constantly and holding it above its body with its two claws. This crab has a rounded carapace and two sturdy pincers which are a delicate pink colour.

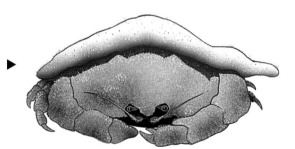

Spiny spider crab - *Maja squinado*

The spinous spider crab has a convex, oval-shaped carapace with a spiny edge. It is a yellow brown colour and has long, lighter-coloured appendages. It is nocturnal, and during the mating season forms large groups near the surface. A similar but smaller species, *Maja verrucosa*, has a carapace covered with algae, sponges and hydrozoans that make it difficult to spot.

BRYOZOANS

False coral - *Myriapora truncata*

It has a branched, erect orange skeleton covered by fine hairs. The colony is comprised of the tentacles of individual specimens located within little holes along the entire skeleton. It is an orange-red colour and is known as false coral. Although it is often confused with coral, the presence of the holes on its skeleton makes it easy to identify. It is common in poorly illuminated areas.

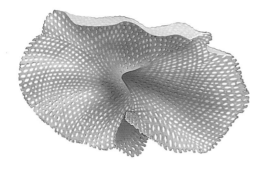

Neptunes' lace- *Sertella septentrionalis*

This is known as sea lace bryozoan. It grows in finely perforated laminae in the form of a cup with fluted edges. Pinkish in colour, it lives in poorly illuminated areas, and despite its hardness, it is quite fragile.

ECHINODERMS

Featherstar - *Antedon mediterranea*

This is commonly known as the crinoid. It has a small, button-shaped body with about ten flexible arms with a group of pinnules on each side. On the other side of its body it has a group of cirri that permit it to grasp onto the substratum. It feeds on suspended particles, which it collects with its arms and brings to its mouth, located in the center of the body and turned upwards, through the movement of small bristles.

Cotton spinner - *Holothuria tubulosa*

The sea cucumber has a tube-shaped body with a mouth at the front end and an anus at the other. The upper portion of the body is scattered with small conical protuberances, while the lower side is traversed by pedicles that permit it to move. It feeds on detritus by swallowing and sifting sediment.

Purple sea star - *Ophidiaster ophidianus*

This is a large red star, with arms that often exceed 20 centimetres in length. The surface of its body appears velvety, and its colour varies from dark red to orange spotted with red. The lower side of the body is lighter, and ambulatory pedicles extend from furrows along the arms.

Red starfish - *Echinaster sepositus*

The is the most common red star. It has a rough body with five arms, sometimes more, which are cylindrical and furrowed on the lower side, from which the pedicles protrude. It feeds on other invertebrates and is common in all environments to over 200 metres deep.

Mediterranean longspined urchin - *Centrostephanus longispinus*

The long-spined urchin is difficult to spot, not because it is rare, but because it is quite reclusive, with nocturnal habits. It lives in dark areas where it inserts itself into cracks with its long tentacles. The upper part of its body has small reddish-purple spines which are in continuous movement.

▶

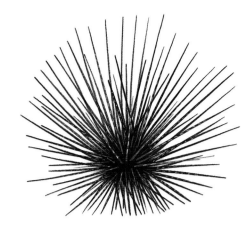

Black sea urchin - *Arbacia lixula*

◀ Totally black in colour, this species is commonly known as the black sea urchin. It grazes on algae in well-illuminated areas, scraping encrusting red algae from the rocks and often grazing the rocks bare.

Violet sea urchin - *Sphaerechinus granularis*

This is known as the whitetip sea urchin. Many specimens have white-tipped spines, while some are totally white. It is almost spherical in form and is common on meadows of Neptune grass, on which rhizomes and roots it feeds.

▶

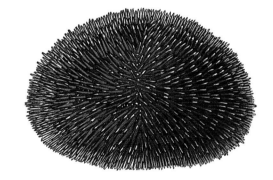

Stony seaurchin - *Paracentrotus lividus*

This is known as the stony sea urchin. Its colour may vary from brown, green to dark violet-blue, and it is common in well illuminated areas, where it grazes on algae with soft thalli.
◀ As it does not like the light, however, it covers its body with fragments of algae and other objects, and is thus easily distinguishable from *Arbacia lixula*.

Purple heart urchin - *Spatangus purpureus*

This is a heart urchin which by day lives buried in the sediment. Its exoskeleton has an ovoid, heart-shaped form covered with a fine pale purple fuzz, from which grow a few longer, thin spines. Like all heart urchins, it feeds by gathering edible matter from the sediment, separating it from inorganic matter. ▶

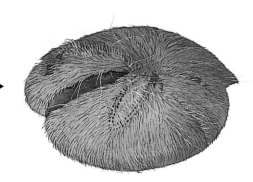

TUNICATES

Light bulb sea squirt - *Clavelina lepadiformis*

This is a colonial ascidian. The colony is formed by various individuals joined by a common stolon at the base. Each individual is connected to the stolon by a peduncle, surmounted by a transparent body with two characteristic orifices. It is quite common on rocky seabeds in late spring, and can form large groups. It feeds by filtering organic material.

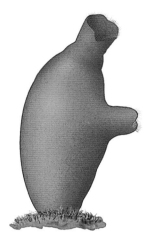

Red sea squirt - *Halocinthya papillosa*

This is a solitary ascidian with a characteristic bright red colour. Also known as the sea potato, it has a thick, rough tunic and is quite sensitive to light and movement, withdrawing rapidly. It is very common in all environments with dim light. It reproduces sexually.

FISH

Common stingray - *Dasyatis pastinaca*

This is a cartilaginous fish with a characteristic rhomboidal form with a long, tapered tail with a serrated spine used as a defensive weapon. Known as the stingray, it lives on the sea floor, often covered with sediment from detrital or sandy seabeds. It feeds on various creatures, and captures fish, crustaceans and mollusks.

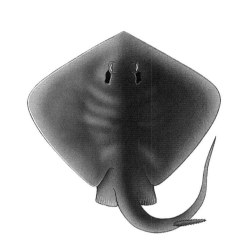

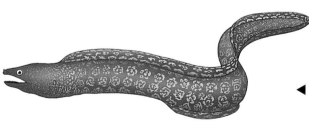

Mediterranean moray - *Murena helena*

One of the most common fish, the moray is wrongly considered ferocious and dangerous. It lives in crevices from which only the front portion of its body protrudes. It comes out to hunt only at night and feeds primarily on octopuses, but also on fish and crustaceans. Its mouth is always wide open, showing its teeth, in order to oxygenate its gills.

Conger eel - *Conger conger*

The conger eel has a tapered body which is a uniform grey colour, and it may reach quite large dimensions. By day it lives hidden in crevices among the rocks, and it is quite common around sunken ships. By night it comes out of its lair to hunt, feeding primarily on fish. One of its principal reproduction areas is the very deep waters to the southeast of Sardinia.

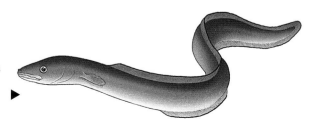

Forkbeard - *Phycis phycis*

The forkbeard is common in dark areas. It is a member of the cod family and can easily be distinguished by the two barbels below the mouth and its ventral fins in the form of a forked filament, which has a tactile function. It has two dorsal fins; the second dorsal fin and the anal fin are symmetrical and extend to the tail.

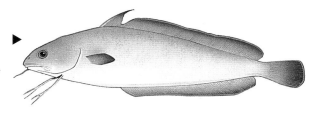

John dory - *Zeus faber*

The John Dory has an unmistakable appearance: its body, compressed at the sides, is oval and surmounted by the extremely long rays of the dorsal fin. Its ventral and anal fins are also quite generous. It has a very large mouth which is turned upward and can be extroverted. It is a yellowish silvery colour with a large dark spot in the form of an ocellus. According to legend, the spot is the mark left by the hand of St. Peter.

Sea horse - *Hippocampus guttulatus*

The easily recognizable seahorse usually lives with its tail gripping algae, invertebrates or leaves of Neptune grass. It swims slowly in an erect position, frenetically agitating its transparent dorsal fin. The male incubates and hatches the eggs in a ventral sac. It always appears unkempt and sad.

Red Scorpionfish - *Scorpaena scrofa*

The red scorpionfish is characterized by a large head followed by two broad pectoral fins and a stubby body. Its head is full of leaf-shaped protuberances, which along with its colour increase the general mimetic effect. The spines of its dorsal fin and the operculum can emit a powerful poison which can cause intense pain. The poison is thermolabile, and immersion of the injured part into warm water relieves the pain.

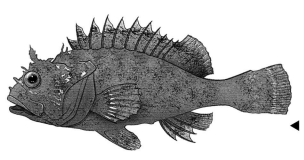

Dusky grouper - *Epinephelus marginatus*

The grouper can become quite large. Its body is often very broad, and although it rarely exceeds a metre in length, it can weigh more than 50 kilograms. It often hovers vertically, slowly moving its wide pectoral fins. It takes shelter in deep, complex lairs. Younger individuals are female, while after sexual inversion older specimens become male.

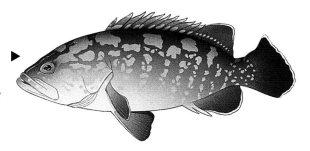

Comber - *Serranus cabrilla*

The comber is quite common in all environments. It has a prominent mandible and a brown-striped body. It is a hermaphrodite species, possessing both male and female gonads which are active at the same time. It has not yet been determined whether it is self-fertilizing.

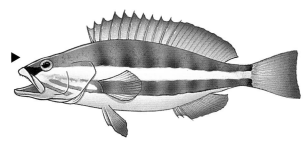

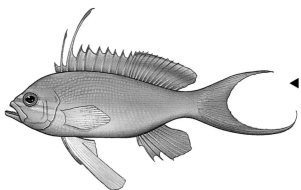

Painted comber - *Serranus scriba*

The painted comber or sea perch is brightly coloured. Its head is streaked with a network of red and blue lines, and its back has dark stripes alternating with yellow. It has a very evident light blue spot on its stomach. It often follows the movements of octopuses and is thus an indicator of their presence. It is hermaphroditic and feeds on small fish and crustaceans.

European seabass - *Dicentrarchus labrax*

The sea bass is a swift predator with an elongated, silvery body. It can become quite large, up to a metre in length. Reproduction takes place in winter, when groups of males fertilize the eggs of a single female. The sea bass adapts well to brackish waters as well, and thus is easy to breed.

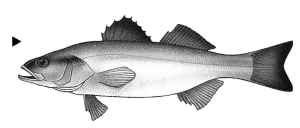

Swallowtail seaperch - *Anthias anthias*

The swallowtail sea perch lives in large schools on deep reefs and in coralligenous areas. As it increases in size it changes sex from female to male. Usually it forms groups of females with a single dominant male. The species exhibits clear sexual dimorphism, with males being more brightly coloured with longer fins.

Cardinal fish - *Apogon imberbis*

The cardinal fish is a small red fish with large dark eyes striped with white. It lives in sizable groups in dark areas, in caves and under rocky masses. Reproduction takes place by means of a sort of coupling in which the eggs are fecundated by means of the fins. The male then collects the fertilized eggs and watches over them until they hatch about 8 days later.

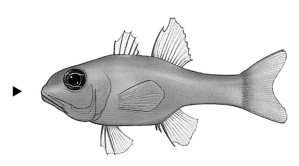

Greater amberjack - *Seriola dumerilli*

The amberjack is a sizable pelagic predator which lives in large schools. It exhibits the homochromy typical of pelagic fish: the upper portion of its body is dark, while the lower portion is light. A dark streak runs diagonally across its head. Young individuals are a bright yellow-gold colour.

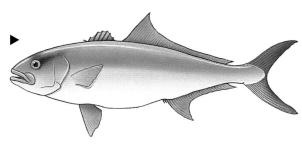

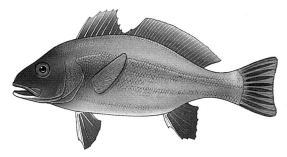

Brown meagre - *Sciaena umbra*

The brown meagre is a common fish in dark areas: it lives in small groups in caves among rocky masses. It has a characteristic brownish bronze colour and the edges of its fins are gold. The first dorsal fin is quite elongated. It can make sounds which are often quite audible underwater.

Striped red mullet - *Mullus surmuletus*

The striped red mullet is easily recognizable by the brick red band that runs the length of its body and the two barbels under its mouth. The two appendages have a sensory function and are utilized to identify the small invertebrates on which it feeds.

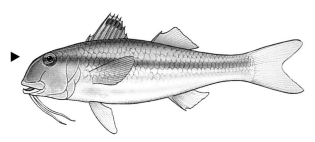

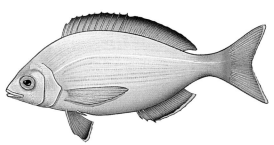

Black seabream - *Spondyliosoma cantharus*

The black seabream is a member of the Sparidae family. It has an oval, compressed body. It usually lives in large groups which can be found in all environments. It is a sequentially hermaphroditic species: it is female when young, while adults are male. It reproduces in the spring, depositing its eggs in sandy areas.

Annular seabream - *Diplodus annularis*

The annular bream is the smallest of this genus, and can be distinguished from the others by its yellowish colour and its elongated oval form. It appears to be a protandrous hermaphrodite: first male and then female. It is common in all environments at shallow depths.

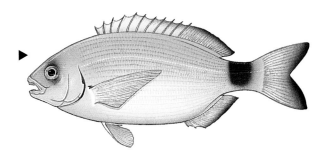

White seabream - *Diplodus sargus*

The white seabream has an oval, silvery body with a black spot on the caudal peduncle. It can reach 50 centimetres in length and has quite large teeth which are capable of crushing the skeleton of sea urchins. It has separate sexes and lives primarily in rocky environments.

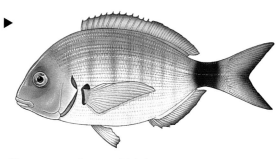

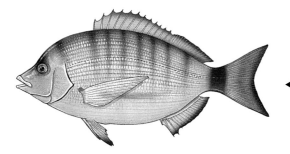

Sharpsnout seabream - *Diplodus puntazzo*

The sharpsnout seabream can easily be distinguished by its pointed snout, its dark vertical stripes, more or less visible, and the dark spot on its caudal peduncle. It is the least sedentary of the seabreams and feeds on both invertebrates and algae.

Common twobanded seabream - *Diplodus vulgaris*

The two-banded seabream is characterized by two black bands on the back of its head and on the caudal peduncle. It can become just as big as the two larger species, but normally it is found in sizable schools of smaller individuals. It is a hermaphroditic species, but there is no precise pattern to its sexual phases.

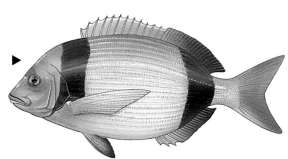

Common dentex - *Dentex dentex*

The dentex is a large pelagic predator which lives in schools near deep reefs. It is silvery with violet blue tones and small turquoise spots. It can become quite large, and the biggest individuals are usually solitary. During the night it often rests on the seabed to sleep, sometimes within caves. It has very large teeth.

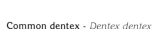

Saddled seabream - *Oblada melanura*

The saddled seabream is silvery with a black spot edged in white located on the caudal peduncle. Its body is elongated and its mouth is turned slightly upwards. It moves in large groups that often hover just a few metres below the surface. It feeds on animals and plants on the seabed and near the surface.

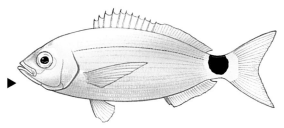

Salema - *Sarpa salpa*

The salema is a classical gregarious fish which is easily distinguished by the golden yellow horizontal stripes that run across it. It has a small mouth which it uses to graze on algae on the seabed or on leaves of Neptune grass. It is a sequential hermaphrodite: first male and then female.

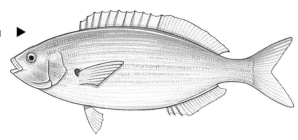

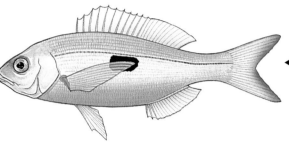

Blotched picarel - *Spicara maena*

The blotched pickerel is a small gregarious fish which normally lives in large schools just a few metres from the surface. It has an elongated body with a black spot in the middle of both sides. It is a sequentially hermaphroditic species: first female and then male. During the reproduction period males become brightly coloured, with azure blue stripes and spots.

Damselfish - *Chromis chromis*

The damselfish is extremely common and can be seen during any dive, in large schools that hover near the surface of the water. Reproduction takes place on the sea floor, where the females deposit the eggs in an area cleaned by the male, who then watches over them until they hatch. Young individuals have an unmistakable electric blue colour.

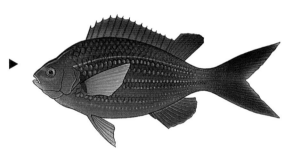

Cockoo wrasse - *Labrus bimaculatus*

This is one of the most colourful wrasses, with an accentuated sexual dimorphism. Females are a light purple-red colour with black and white spots under the dorsal fin. Males are orange with azure stripes over their entire bodies and tails with azure blue edges. It is a sequential hermaphrodite: first female and then male.

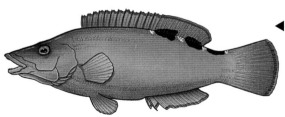

Peacock wrasse - *Symphodus tinca*

The peacock wrasse exhibits evident sexual dimorphism. The smaller females are less colourful, while males have a green and blue snout with dark blue stripes, a yellow body with horizontal blue stripes spotted with red and azure fins with turquoise spots. It is a protandrous hermaphrodite.

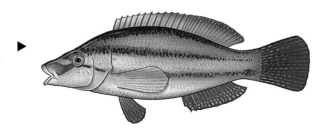

Axillary wrasse - *Symphodus mediterraneus*

The axillary wrasse exhibits sexual differentiation from birth. The sexual dimorphism becomes more accentuated during the reproductive period, when males take on a brick red colour with a noticeably yellow eye and a yellow spot at the base of the pectoral fins. The male builds the nest with algae and detritus and the female deposits her eggs within it.

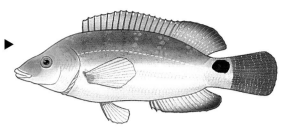

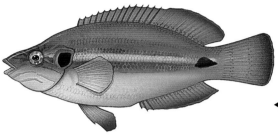

Ocellated wrasse - *Symphodus ocellatus*

The ocellated wrasse takes its name from a characteristic spot behind the eye, green edged with red and azure blue. The male is more colourful than the female, with green and orange stripes on its head and fins. The male uses algae to build a nest, where it watches over the eggs deposited there by the female.

Rainbow wrasse - *Coris julis*

The rainbow wrasse exhibits clear sexual differentiation and is a protogynous hermaphrodite. Females are smaller than males and are a brick red colour on their upper backs with one white and one yellow stripe along their sides. The larger males have a gaudy orange stripe along their sides, with the stomach white in front and green near the tail. Rainbow wrasses are voracious predators and feed on invertebrates.

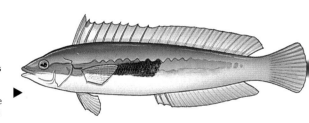

Ornate wrasse - *Thalassoma pavo*

The ornate wrasse is the most "tropical" of the Mediterranean fish due to the three different colour combinations it can assume. A sequential hermaphrodite, its colour varies as it transforms from female to male, with a transition colour as well. The males are the most colourful, with a turquoise head with red stripes, yellow, red and turquoise bands and a red stripe behind the head. The rest of the body is green, with blue fins. It feeds on invertebrates.

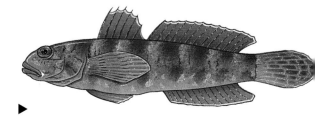

Red mouthed goby - *Gobius cruentatus*

The red-mouthed goby has an elongated body, and like all gobies lives on the seabed. It has two characteristic red spots on its mouth, and a body with brown and white spots. The two dorsal fins are elongated, while the ventral fins form the adhesive disc characteristic of gobies. It feeds primarily on invertebrates.

Slender goby - *Gobius geniporus*

It has the distinctive form of all gobies, with a light-coloured body with dark spots. Its eyes are emerald green. When it lives on the sand or detritus it is quite mimetic and easy to approach. It feeds on invertebrates.

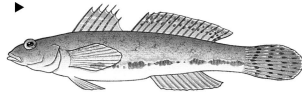

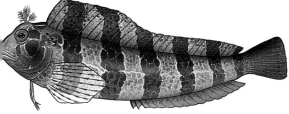

Tompot blenny - *Parablennius gattorugine*

The tompot blenny has a large head with bulging red eyes surmounted by fringed tentacles. The long dorsal fin runs across its elongated body, which has vertical reddish stripes. The two pectoral fins are quite broad and are always spread. It is a territorial species, especially during the reproductive period, when males attempt to have a number of females deposit their eggs in the lair they have selected.

Long striped blenny - *Parablennius rouxi*

This is a small blenny with a white body with a longitudinal dark brown stripe. It has small feathery tentacles on its head. It often lives within holes in the rock or the empty tubes of spirographs, from which only its head protrudes with its two large eyes. It is commonly known as the striped blenny.

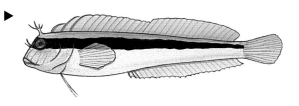

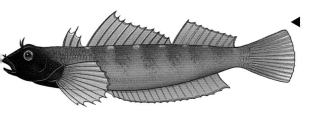

Red blackfaced blenny - *Trypterigion tripteronotus*

The black-faced blenny is a small fish that always lives in contact with the seabed. It has an elongated body with a pointed head. During the reproductive period males are quite colourful, with bright red bodies and black heads; they perform complicated courting rituals to attract females. It feeds on invertebrates.

European barracuda - *Sphyraena sphyraena*

This barracuda belongs to the same family as the tropical barracudas. It has an elongated body with a pointed head and a prominent jaw with pointed teeth. It can become quite large, but usually it is seen in schools of dozens of medium-sized individuals. It is a swift predator and feeds on fish, mollusks and crustaceans.

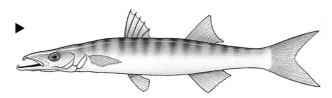

EPILOGUE: A BOOK OF DREAMS FOR PROTECTED AREAS

168 A group of dolphins (Tursiops truncatus) swims near the island of Tavolara on a day when the water is calm. The elusive bottle-nose dolphins are the most common cetaceans along the Sardinian coast.

Writing a guide to scuba diving in Sardinia necessarily leads to a paradox: the most popular diving area for many enthusiasts who choose Sardinia for their diving is in France - in Corsica, to be exact! During the summer months, dozens of boats and hundreds of divers crowd Lavezzi Reef (now known as "grouper reef") every day, coming from a broad stretch of the Sardinian coast from Porto Rotundo to beyond Santa Teresa di Gallura. The island of Lavezzi, just a few miles from the islands of the La Maddalena archipelago, has for many years been a protected area, where constant and attentive control, gentle but well-aimed restrictions and a favorable environment have created an underwater situation that only three or four other areas in the Mediterranean can offer. The only difference between Lavezzi Reef and Sardinia is the far-sightedness of those involved in environmental protection in Corsica and France.

But now a new season has begun in Sardinia as well: the dream of opening the national parks of La Maddalena, the Gulf of Orosei and Asinara, as well as the marine reserves of Capo Caccia, Tavolara, Sinis and Capo Carbonara, has become a reality, and marine parks have actually been created where scuba diving and its related tourism will be natural developments.

It is hoped that this book will make a small, concrete contribution of knowledge that will encourage the development of a network of protected marine areas and a tourist industry compatible with the use and conservation of the extraordinary marine environments that surround the island.